May God Keep You Strong !

Apostle J.Q. Lockett

THE
FREEDOM *of*
FORGIVENESS

Healing Pains of The Past

APOSTLE J.Q. LOCKETT

ISBN: 978-1-7372246-8-6

Publishing By:

DemiCo National, LLC

www.DemiCoNational.com

Literary Agent: The Acklin Group

Dedications

To the following, I dedicate this book:

My wife, Dr Hashonah Lockett

my three children, Nicholas, Jade and Amber Lockett,

my three grandchildren, Jayden, J'adore and Khalil

my parents, the late Edward & Dorothy Lockett,

my sisters, Roselyn Lockett & Sheridan Crawford, my brother, the late Tony Lockett, my sister, the late Cynthia Harris,

and

Grace Church of Stone Mountain &

Miracle Revival Assemblies Fellowship family

Sincerely,
Apostle J.Q. Lockett

TABLE OF CONTENTS

FORWARD

It is so ironic that the Apostle deals with a universal principle that leads to freedom. Read this book and it will change your life. You and I have heard it said, "Sticks and stones may break your bones, but words will never hurt you". The Lord Jesus said, "know the truth and the truth will set you free".

People use words and intentions as weapons to inflict harm physically and emotionally. We were created to function with norms to provide ethical relationships in our communities. When we are assaulted emotionally for whatever reason, for the moment, our hearts-spirits are in free fall. Some have withdrawn and committed suicide, others some heinous act of harm even the murder of another. There is no telling where we end up when we fail to forgive.

Pain is not an ally, and a bruise is not easily removed. It takes time to heal. There are so many people who never heal because they are fragile. Hurt people, hurt people. Behind every action there is an equal and opposite reaction.

Our hearts produces enzymes that affect our white and red blood cells. We were given life in order to cultivate positive relationships. It is essential to see each other as essential workers in finding a hurt and heal it and finding a need to fill it. We are our brother's keeper, and we need to protect each other from internal, physiological, psychological, and spiritual injuries that can cause a soul to be marred eternally.

We have all said things that have interacted adversely but God 's Grace is amazing, and He provides us the opportunity to turn the page.

This book will help you understand forgiveness as essential to the soul as breathing is to life. The cry of the Lord Jesus for those who were crucifying him is essential for all who would be like him to live with him. He said on the cross when being maligned and crucified "Father forgive them for they not what they do". Implicit in that statement also is that they do not know who they are doing it to. Whether good or bad, "when you have done this to the least of these you have done it unto me." Forgiveness produces freedom. Freedom for the persecuted and the perpetrator. "Whenever we free others we free ourselves. I am forgiven therefore I must forgive. Thanks Apostle Jeffrey Q. Lockett for releasing others to a place where they can now breathe, live, and have a good night's rest.

Archbishop LeRoy Bailey Jr.

The First Cathedral of Bloomfield, Connecticut

FORWARD

Apostle Jeffrey Lockett is an emerging, sage thought leader transcending the barriers between the faith-based community and the marketplace. I have known this man through seasons and have found him to be a man of faith, honor, and respect. He has a genuine passion to pursue his call clearly evidenced in the leadership skills he has exercised throughout his tenure of service in the Kingdom of God. Supported by an incredible wife, children, and grandchildren, he makes a powerful case for the presentation of this published work.

In this volume, Lockett approaches the most inclusive dynamic of all time, the issue of forgiveness.

The season in which this book is released unimpeachably ratifies its necessity and critical approach to one of humanity's pressing, chronic, and acute spiritual pathogens.

Addressing this topic in a pragmatic and diagnostic manner, Lockett provides an easy-to-understand spectrum of the causes, symptoms, and challenges associated with this issue. He skillfully and with deft application of the Word of God ushers readers to a practical pathway to solutions to disenfranchise the stronghold that is unforgiveness.

Dealing with many of the common denials and delusions that accompany people wrestling with forgiveness, the Author probes the anatomy of how forgiveness works to relieve people from typical misunderstandings to lifelong strongholds that rob people of peace, dignity, and meaning of purpose in life.

Death is not the worst event in life, but rather life without a purpose. The issue of forgiveness can hibernate under years of bitterness, resentment, and unresolved offenses resulting in the deprivation of many from the talents, abilities, and gifts God grants to those who have been severely hindered and/or have succumbed to an unwillingness to forgive.

The Freedom of Forgiveness will help guide you on a pathway to fulfillment of your God given purpose.

By all means, share it with all that you know and don't know!

Dr. Joseph M. Ripley

The Body of Christ Church Intl., Atlanta, Georgia

INTRODUCTION

All our lives we have been fed a million clichés on forgiveness. We've heard thousands of fairy tales, seen hundreds of movies, and even listened to dozens of songs all encouraging forgiveness of those who have wronged us. One would think that after so much content urging us to practice forgiveness that by the time we reach adulthood, we would have strengthened our forgiveness muscle. Unfortunately, we all know that the forgiveness muscle is often the most difficult muscle in the human mental anatomy to strengthen.

Since antiquity, forgiveness has been practiced. Forgiveness is a Biblical principle, going back to Adam and Eve. Forgiveness for salvation and for fellowship with God is practiced by today's believers. Receiving salvation from our Heavenly Father for mankind's original sin, and for sins prior to salvation is the redemption found in making Jesus Lord in one's life. Confession of sins to God that occur after salvation, is how believers maintain fellowship with God. In-addition, the truth regarding forgiving and forgetting, and the relationship that forgiveness has with healing is also found in The Bible. As glorious as it sounds, we all know that forgiveness is not an easy task by any means. Why is forgiveness so difficult?

The answer is simple. We forget how easy forgiveness is. The lessons of forgiveness never change, but we do. Forgiveness is not complicated, we are complicated. So, first we must stop blaming forgiveness for our mental and spiritual hang-ups and place the blame where it belongs, on the human mind. Hopefully we are changing for the better, but that's not always the case. We forget that we are all works in progress, all the time. Physically, mentally, and spiritually, all of us are going through change. We forget how change makes us vulnerable to mistakes. We forget what we have been forgiven for. Furthermore, we forget to be patient with one another. We forget that as adults, deep down inside, we all are like children, and all need the same love and tenderness a child receives by forgiveness. Most of all, we forget to be humble like children, and be willing to admit our mistakes. One of the hardest things to do is take accountability for the bad things we have done. Big hurts caused by others or by us can cause a lot of confusion and inner turmoil resulting in lack of trust, and unforgiveness can be fatal.

Failing to forgive, or unforgiveness, is the practice of engaging in endless thoughts of anger, vengeance, hate, and resentment that have unproductive outcomes for oneself, such as increased anxiety, depression, elevated blood pressure, vascular resistance, decreased immune response, and worse outcomes in coronary artery disease. Practicing forgiveness enables the transgressed individual to reduce their engagement in rumination thus reducing their experience of anger, resentment, and hate.

Truthfully, I admit that it can be easy to forgive someone quickly for a small offense, but if someone has committed a serious offense against you, the process may take months or even years. It's not the act of saying words of forgiveness that is beneficial, it's the intention behind the words. Before you can forgive, it's important to have processed or reflected on the offense. What happened, how did it make you feel, and how has the anger or hurt you've experienced affected you since? It can be helpful to try to empathize. If you can put yourself in the shoes of the person who hurt you, you may better understand why they did what they did. This doesn't excuse the offense or the offender, but it can help you see the person more as a human being who made a mistake. Acknowledging that you have sometimes hurt other people and have been forgiven can also help you learn to forgive others.

As I invite you to take this journey with me into the construct of forgiveness, I want to first let you know what to expect. You have my word. I won't throw a truck load of old clichés your way that probably have no more meaning to you anymore than the *Itsy-Bitsy Spider*. I won't insult your injury. I ask that you take a deep breath and relax as we peel back the mental, spiritual, and physical layers of forgiveness and how to truly utilize this gift as a skill to accomplishing our purpose in God.

CHAPTER ONE

All the Ways in Which We Never Healed

There are many different types of traumas that we experience in this journey called life and if you are not careful to understand how each plays a part in your daily life, then you may never truly develop your gift of forgiveness. Yes, I said gift. Forgiveness is a gift. It is one of the most precious gifts that God has given us to heal us and one another. However, if we fail to acknowledge all the ways in which we never healed, then we can never apply forgives to all the areas that await our forgiveness before we can truly align with God. In this chapter I would like to focus on community healing. Community healing deals with the healing of an entire community, not just one individual.

That community may be a family, city, town, race, political party, or even a religion. If we can agree we all know of communities that are in great need of healing from past wounds, then we have to also acknowledge the need for community forgiveness. Community forgiveness—and on a larger scale, societal forgiveness—is a collective decision to change negative behavior, thoughts, feelings, and motivations toward an offending group or groups of people. Community injustices vary greatly in their nature. Some affect a small portion of the community; others touch the lives of virtually all members. Some community offenses are minor, and others are quite severe, even life-threatening. As such, community forgiveness is a process that unfolds within a particular place and time. Believers are aware that each person can receive the forgiveness of his sins, through the death and resurrection of Jesus, but what about nations who have transgressed against other nations? What about races who have enslaved other races? To help answer this question I must introduce another word of study to our forgiveness journey.

Another term, which is also used often when speaking of forgiveness, is "atonement". Most believers have heard that term as well – however, many people think that atonement is exactly the same thing as forgiveness. In other words, many people believe that the terms "forgiveness" and "atonement" are synonyms. While there are some similarities between those two terms in Scripture. Both forgiveness and atonement have to do with sin – i.e., they both deal with sins that people have committed. However, that does not necessarily indicate that the meanings of those two terms are *identical*. So, let's investigate Scripture, to determine if there are any *differences* between forgiveness and atonement.

In several places, Scripture links our forgiveness through Christ, with the Passover festival in the Old Testament. In other words, Scripture associates Jesus with the lamb that was killed on Passover – and it also indicates that because Jesus is our "Passover lamb", we can now obtain *forgiveness* of our sins. For example, consider these passages:

John 1:29 (ESV):
29Â The next day he [John the Baptist] saw Jesus coming toward him, and said, Behold, the Lamb of God, who takes away the sin of the world!

1 Corinthians 5:7 (ESV):
7Â Cleanse out the old leaven that you may be a new lump, as you really are unleavened. For Christ, our Passover lamb, has been sacrificed.
As shown above, our forgiveness in Christ is "associated" with the Passover festival. As a result, it appears likely that we can obtain additional information about the meaning of forgiveness, if we investigate further into the Passover festival.

Of course, that leaves one other question – how can we obtain additional information about the meaning of atonement? As it turns out, there is *another* festival in the Old Testament which explicitly deals with atonement. That festival is actually called– the Day of Atonement. Let's break down the Passover and Day of Atonement festivals. First, consider the passage below, which contains information about the actions taken during the Passover.

Exodus 12:3-13 (ESV):

[3] Tell all the congregation of Israel that on the tenth day of this month every man shall take a lamb according to their fathers' houses, a lamb for a household. [4] And if the household is too small for a lamb, then he and his nearest neighbor shall take according to the number of persons; according to what each can eat you shall make your count for the lamb. [5] Your lamb shall be without blemish, a male a year old. You may take it from the sheep or from the goats, [6] and you shall keep it until the fourteenth day of this month, when the whole assembly of the congregation of Israel shall kill their lambs at twilight.

[7] Then they shall take some of the blood and put it on the two doorposts and the lintel of the houses in which they eat it. [8] They shall eat the flesh that night, roasted on the fire; with unleavened bread and bitter herbs they shall eat it. [9] Do not eat any of it raw or boiled in water, but roasted, its head with its legs and its inner parts. [10] And you shall let none of it remain until the morning; anything that remains until the morning you shall burn. [11] In this manner you shall eat it: with your belt fastened, your sandals on your feet, and your staff in your hand. And you shall eat it in haste. It is the Lord's Passover. [12] For I will pass through the land of Egypt that night, and I will strike all the firstborn in the land of Egypt, both man and beast; and on all the gods of Egypt I will execute judgments: I am the Lord. [13] The blood shall be a sign for you, on the houses where you are. And when I see the blood, I will pass over you, and no plague will befall you to destroy you, when I strike the land of Egypt.

The Passover is focused on individuals. Every individual person must eat from their household's Passover lamb; and every individual home must have the blood of the household's Passover lamb placed on its doorposts. The Passover does not involve sacrifices from the people. Each family does kill a lamb during The Passover – but then the people, themselves, eat that lamb. In other words, the people do not really "give up" anything to God on Passover. The Passover does not require any hardships for people. In other words, people do not need to undergo any sort of "difficulties" or "afflictions" on The Passover. Christ is called our "Passover lamb". So, let's compare the forgiveness that we receive through Christ, with the forgiveness listed in the Passover. Forgiveness through Christ is focused on individuals – exactly like Passover. Basically, each and every individual needs to come to Christ, in order to have his or her own sins forgiven. In other words, forgiveness has *nothing to do* with the community at large.

Forgiveness through Christ does not require sacrifices from the people – just like Passover. Jesus died for us on the cross – so that we do not need to die, in order to be forgiven of our sins. In fact, we are not even required to "sacrifice" our money or resources to be forgiven. (Of course, believers are *strongly* exhorted to be generous with their resources – but donating "x" amount of money is not a requirement of forgiveness.) Forgiveness through Christ does not require hardships for the people – again, similar to Passover. Basically, people do not need to "afflict" themselves to be forgiven. For example, people do not need to go on difficult fasts, or to become ascetic monks, to be forgiven. (Of course, it is true that believers will often be *persecuted*, simply because of their faith. However, that persecution is not a requirement of forgiveness – i.e., a believer will not be "denied" forgiveness if he does not get persecuted.)

Our forgiveness through Christ mirrors in many ways the forgiveness listed in the Passover. Not only that, but Jesus precisely "matched" many of the *other* items in Passover as well – such as, He was a lamb "without spot or blemish" (i.e., He was without sin); and according to Biblical references, He died at 3 PM – which was the exact same time that the Passover lambs began being slaughtered. When we explore the meaning of atonement in the Bible, it doesn't take very long to realize that atonement deals with the all-important issue of substitution. But honestly, the implications associated with atonement and substitution will likely only confuse us, and possibly even trouble us, unless we understand the larger picture of God's story.

Even in the beginning of God's story, we are told that God created a good world (Gen. 1:12, Gen. 1:18, Gen 1:21, Gen 1:25, Gen. 1:31) for his people to enjoy. God's good design involved placing his mark on a people who would experience intimate fellowship with him as they worked alongside the Designer to saturate the universe with his glory (Habakkuk 2:14).
From the very beginning, the eternal plan was for image bearers (Genesis 1:26) to represent God and his mission. Not only were the borders of the Garden of Eden to be ever extending, but humankind was to image their Creator by undertaking the responsibility of causing creation to flourish.
The idea of "cultivating" (Gen. 2:5, Gen. 2:15) implies the development of culture in such areas as art, music, government, technology, agriculture and

so forth. It is no coincidence that the trajectory of God's creative work begins in a garden but culminates in the "holy city" (Revelation 21:2).

Adam decides that he is more capable than God of defining what is good from what is evil (Genesis 3:5). As a result of Adam's mutiny, all of creation is cast into a dark curse (Romans 8:20), and God's good world plunges into a bottomless chaos from which only the Creator will be able to rescue. It is critical to our understanding of atonement to grasp the full measure of Adam's choice and its implications on all of humanity in every generation. Because God is holy and perfectly pure, the Bible says he "drove the man out" (Genesis 3:24) due to Adam's sin. But because Adam represented all of man throughout all of time, when he was driven from God's presence, so were we driven from our Maker's side. Man's greatest need now becomes the necessity to be brought back into God's presence where we were always meant to be, but now there is a barrier of sin that separates us from God (Isaiah 59:2).

At this point in human history, we must confess that God would have been justified to eradicate humanity from his good world. And if God would have preferred such a course of resolution, no man could have cried, "unfair!" After all, does not the potter have a right over the clay (Romans 9:19-22)? To this conclusion, however, the Maker was not so inclined. It is precisely at this point in the story that grace emerges and provides the backdrop against which God's merciful redemptive plan is set into motion.

Genesis 12 provides for us a more detailed glimpse into the salvific intentions, which up to this point in Scripture have only been alluded to. It is here that we discover how God will choose one family to be the very instrument through which "every tongue, tribe, and nation" (Revelation 5:9) will be brought back into God's presence to continue the work which Adam was intended to fulfill before his betrayal. It is the family of Abram and his descendent, Israel, which foreshadow spiritual Israel, the church (Romans 2:28-29; Galatians 3:7-9), who will take up the mantle of Adam to bless all the families of the earth (Genesis 12:1-3).

Nevertheless, the dilemma of sin still remains. God has chosen a people to represent him and move his mission forward, but the people are infected and warped by iniquity. Where once, prior to the fall, God's presence was a place of peace, joy, and safety, it has now become a place of danger and terror because God's holiness will burn up anything impure and unclean that attempts to break through the perimeter (Exodus 33:20; Leviticus 16:1-2). How will God reinstate, use, and draw near to a sinful people without destroying them? The answer is found in *atonement*.

The Day of Atonement portrays a crucially vital ritual in the worship practices of Israel, not merely because of Israel's present need but also because of what the act of atonement prefigures. In response to the arrogant attempt of Nadab and Abihu to enter Yahweh's presence on their own terms and their ensuing deaths (Leviticus 10:1-3), their father, Aaron is warned not to act as presumptuously as his sons, or he will meet the same fate. It is in God's instruction to Aaron that we see atonement defined (Leviticus 16).

The word, *atonement,* means "to cover over one's debt," and this act of covering will be symbolically acted out as Aaron the priest sacrifices two male goats before Yahweh. One goat will be slaughtered for a sin offering as a substitute in the place of sinful man. Rather than man paying the price of death for his sin, the goat's blood is spilled instead. What a breath-taking image.

The second goat suffers a different, though no less poignant, fate as it becomes a *scapegoat* (Leviticus 16:8, 22) in which the sins of Israel are, again symbolically, placed on the goat prior to the animal being led deep into the wilderness from which it will never return. This signals what the Psalmist explicitly proclaims when he says, "As far as the east is from the west, so far has he removed our transgressions from us." (Psalm 103:12) Though such practices may seem barbaric to modern ears, blood was essential for atonement because "the life of the flesh is in the blood" (Leviticus 17:11). In essence, the life-giving blood of the sacrifice is substituted for the death payment required at the hands of the one who has offended God. Sin can never be overlooked or ignored. God does not simply turn a blind eye to our offense. Someone has to die.

Leviticus 23:26-27:
"The Lord spoke to Moses, saying, "On exactly the tenth day of this seventh month is the day of atonement; it shall be a holy convocation for you, and you shall humble your souls and present an offering by fire to the Lord."

Leviticus 16:5,7-10,21-22,29-34 (ESV):

5ᴬ And he [Aaron] shall take from the congregation of the people of Israel two male goats for a sin offering, and one ram for a burnt offering.

7ᴬ Then he shall take the two goats and set them before the Lord at the entrance of the tent of meeting. 8ᴬ And Aaron shall cast lots over the two goats, one lot for the Lord and the other lot for Azazel. 9ᴬ And Aaron shall present the goat on which the lot fell for the Lord and use it as a sin offering, 10ᴬ but the goat on which the lot fell for Azazel shall be presented alive before the Lord to make atonement over it, that it may be sent away into the wilderness to Azazel.

21ᴬ And Aaron shall lay both his hands on the head of the live goat, and confess over it all the iniquities of the people of Israel, and all their transgressions, all their sins. And he shall put them on the head of the goat and send it away into the wilderness by the hand of a man who is in readiness. 22ᴬ The goat shall bear all their iniquities on itself to a remote area, and he shall let the goat go free in the wilderness. 29ᴬ And it shall be a statute to you forever that in the seventh month, on the tenth day of the month, you shall afflict yourselves and shall do no work, either the native or the stranger who sojourns among you. 30ᴬ For on this day shall atonement be made for you to cleanse you. You shall be clean before the Lord from all your sins. 31ᴬ It is a Sabbath of solemn rest to you, and you shall afflict yourselves; it is a statute forever. 32ᴬ And the priest who is anointed and consecrated as priest in his father's place shall make atonement, wearing the holy linen garments. 33ᴬ He shall make atonement for the holy sanctuary, and he shall make atonement for the tent of meeting and for the altar, and he shall make atonement for the priests and for all the people of the assembly. ^{34Â} *And this shall be a statute forever for you, that atonement may be made for the people of Israel once in the year because of all their sins. And Aaron did as the Lord commanded Moses.*

Numbers 29:7-11 (ESV):

^{7Â} *On the tenth day of this seventh month you shall have a holy convocation and afflict yourselves. You shall do no work,* ^{8Â} *but you shall offer a burnt offering to the Lord, a pleasing aroma: one bull from the herd, one ram, seven male lambs a year old: see that they are without blemish.* ^{9Â} *And their grain offering shall be of fine flour mixed with oil, three tenths of an ephah for the bull, two tenths for the one ram,* ^{10Â} *a tenth for each of the seven lambs:* ^{11Â} *also one male goat for a sin offering, besides the sin offering of atonement, and the regular burnt offering and its grain offering, and their drink offerings.*

The Day of Atonement is focused on the community. The entire community of Israel gathers for the festival; and then a single goat – the "scapegoat" – is used to make atonement for the entire community. The Day of Atonement does involve sacrifices from the people. Four different types of animals – as well as flour and oil – are offered up to God on the Day of Atonement. Those sacrifices are "burnt" offerings – meaning that they are *completely* consumed by fire. The Day of Atonement does require hardships for the people. The community is instructed to "afflict" themselves on the Day of Atonement. Among other things, this means that there is a community-wide fast – i.e., it is forbidden to consume any food or water on that day.

As mentioned previously, Passover is associated with our forgiveness, and of course the Day of Atonement deals with atonement. As a result, based upon all of the above information, the following conclusions can be drawn about the "forgiveness" and "atonement" concepts:

Forgiveness is based on each individual's actions; it does not involve sacrificing people's items to God; and it does not require people to undergo physical hardships. Atonement is based on the community's actions; it does involve sacrificing people's items to God; and it requires people to undergo physical hardships. Basically, besides the fact that both terms deal with sin, forgiveness and atonement are almost complete opposites of each other!

The Day of Atonement arguably highlights one of the most important rituals in the Bible, and ironically, it is set forth and explained in one of the most overlooked and neglected books in the Bible by most Christians today. In Leviticus 16, Moses records Yahweh's instructions regarding the manner in which Aaron is to enter the holy place to sacrifice before the Lord to make "atonement" the sins of himself and Israel. Rather than being an obscure and isolated Old Testament principle, atonement becomes a visible display of God's fierce commitment to redeem his people and through which the future redemption of God's people is to be comprehended.

As the blood is sprinkled in the tabernacle and on the mercy seat, man is once again ushered into the garden-presence of his Creator, but only temporarily. This scene will need to be reenacted time and time again until a more permanent sacrifice is offered. Even today, Jews around the world celebrate the most holy day called Yom Kippur, which is The Day of Atonement. Though Jewish sacrifices ended in AD 70 with the destruction of the temple, Orthodox Jews continue to give careful observance during this 10-day, holy festival known as Yom Kippur. Yom Kippur is observed by feasting, fasting, wearing white garments, and prescribed prayers as the worshippers seek God's forgiveness and cleansing from their sin. Christians, of course, do not celebrate Yom Kippur, but we do revel in the accomplishment of atonement once and for all by the one, true Lamb that all other bleeding lambs pointed to. On the cross, at the very same moment that a Jewish priest would have been cutting the throat of a woolen lamb, the Heavenly Father, who loves His family too much to see them destroyed, was "causing the iniquity of us all" (Isaiah 53:6) to fall on Jesus His Son.

Now let's connect the dots back to all the ways in which we never healed. Let's take a moment to address the elephant in the room. As a black man, I cannot proceed forth without sharing insight into all the ways that the black community, white community, Christian community, and the entire United States never healed from slavery. Yes, I did include the Christian community because we are in a downward spiral of more and more African Americans each year who turn from Christianity because of the misuse of the religion during slavery. Every day we witness further evidence of situations on local and national scales in which we never healed from slavery. Let's just be frank. The black community as a whole, has yet to forgive America for hundreds of years of trauma. Now, while I do believe that national growth is dependent upon America facing the music of its dark past, we as a people cannot delay our healing and social and emotional advancement waiting on atonement. Christ covered atonement. We may never see our forty acres and a mule. We may never see reparations. If America decides to extend such acts to the black community, then fine, however, we deny the atonement of Christ's sacrifice by asking for further atonement from a nation.

The legacy of slavery still resonates for many Americans, according to a Pew Research Center survey conducted in 2019, with 63% believing it affects the position of black people in American society today either a great deal or a fair amount. Black adults are particularly likely to say slavery continues to have an impact: More than eight-in-ten say this is the case, including 59% who say the legacy of slavery affects the situation of black people a great deal. By comparison, 26% of whites, 29% of Hispanics and 33% of Asians say slavery affects the position of black people in American society today a great deal, though majorities of each group say it does so at least a fair amount.

Let us remember that forgiveness does not require forgetting the past but learning from the past. You're not letting anyone off the hook by forgiving them. In fact, we don't have a hook to keep them on, God does. Forgiveness realigns our souls back with God's original plan before wrong or sin occurred. Just as when forgave Adam, it set Adam back in alignment with God. Yes, Adam still had consequences, but He was returned to a space of clarity with God. We will never possess true clarity from God still wearing lens of unforgiveness.

If we take a closer look at how the black family was dismantled during slavery and post slavery, and then forgive those wretched wrongs, we can find strategy to reunifying the black family unit. All of America has to face the music that we never healed. America will lack healing until it forgives itself, and the black community will lack healing until we forgive America.

CHAPTER TWO

12 Signs of Unforgiveness

Forgiveness means giving up hope for a different past. It means knowing that the past is over, the dust has settled, and the destruction left in its wake can never be reconstructed to resemble what it was. It's accepting that there's no magic solution to the damage that's been caused. It's the realization that as unfair as the hurricane was, you still have to live in its city of ruins. And no amount of anger is going to reconstruct that city. You have to do it yourself. Forgiveness means accepting responsibility – not for causing the destruction, but for cleaning it up. It's the decision that restoring your own peace is finally a bigger priority than disrupting someone else's.

You think you're over it. You pretend everything is ok. But something isn't quite right. You have trouble sleeping. You can't stop thinking about what happened. You can't seem to move on. We have a hard time forgiving people, some more than others. The reason is because many of us have faulty notions of what forgiveness is in the first place – like receiving an apology or being reconciled with the person. We may not want to admit it, but sometimes when we're looking to offer forgiveness, we want it to be because somebody else conceded first. But what you're waiting for may never happen, especially when dealing with toxic people. How can you know whether unforgiveness is eating you alive?

Here are some warning signs of unforgiveness. Because your efforts to heal will at times feel like a fight, here are also some counterpunches to help reverse the course of unhealthy behaviors:

1. You're desperate to make them understand how you feel. Does your inner monologue sound like this? "If the person who caused me pain could only see what they'd done, they would want to say they were sorry."

Counterpunch: It's hard to swallow, but the person may never recognize what they've done. Acceptance and letting go are key aspects of forgiveness. A time-tested way to do this is to write them a letter that you do not intend to send. Do this with the ultimate intention of destroying it and letting go of its contents.

Proverbs 3:5-6: [5] *Trust in the Lord with all thine heart; and lean not unto thine own understanding.* [6] *In all thy ways acknowledge him, and he shall direct thy paths.*

2. You're unable to reframe your experiences. When you allow another person to color your memories, the sight of a formerly favorite drink or the smell of a once loved eatery will only bring you angst. The pleasant associations you once had are gone.

Counterpunch: Acknowledge the part this association played in your life but don't allow it to control you going forward. This may mean donating the offending item or hiding it away for a time. It may mean creating new, happy memories with a cherished friend in a place where you once found yourself overwhelmed with negativity.

Philippians 2:1-5: If there be therefore any consolation in Christ, if any comfort of love, if any fellowship of the Spirit, if any bowels and mercies, ² Fulfil ye my joy, that ye be likeminded, having the same love, being of one accord, of one mind.³ Let nothing be done through strife or vainglory; but in lowliness of mind let each esteem other better than themselves.⁴ Look not every man on his own things, but every man also on the things of others.⁵ Let this mind be in you, which was also in Christ Jesus:

3. You're experiencing bursts of anger. If you're struggling with unforgiveness, you're likely bottling up your anger. Oftentimes, the person who is the recipient of the inevitable outburst is not the person who caused the stress or pain.

Counterpunch: Be mindful when you start to feel anger building. Be aware of the source. If you catch yourself in the middle of an outburst, it's never too late to do an about face. Apologize to the victim of your outburst. Take a deep breath. If you can, spend a few moments alone.

James 1:20: ²⁰ For the wrath of man worketh not the righteousness of God.

4. You're petty and impulsive. When interacting with the person who you struggle to forgive, do you make snide remarks? Do you send them passive aggressive texts? Do you engage in mudslinging? And yet you're still powerless because you have not forgiven them.

Counterpunch: Pause before engaging with the person. Sometimes a moment is all you need to let your conscience kick in. Is your contemplated interaction going to improve things, or just take the edge off of your hurt for a moment before the regret comes?

Psalm 31:7: *⁷ I will be glad and rejoice in thy mercy: for thou hast considered my trouble; thou hast known my soul in adversities;*

5. You're erratic and compulsive. You can't control the hurtful person, but you can control your environment. This can quickly become a negative spiral of compulsive activity. Maybe for you this means keeping your spaces spotless, checking social media repeatedly, or making unnecessary purchases. Maybe it involves comfort eating. These behaviors give you the impression of being in control, but they will not change the result of your interactions with the person. These activities only distract you from getting to the heart of the problem.

Counterpunch: During compulsive behavior, there is often a moment when you realize what is happening. Choose to pull away. What is important to you? Is it being reflected in the way you spend your time? Is what you're doing helping you to heal?

Proverbs 25:28: [28] *He that hath no rule over his own spirit is like a city that is broken down, and without walls.*

6. You hate yourself. I know, this may be a bit strong. But it's probably not far from the truth. If you're stuck in unforgiveness, you are probably experiencing a toxic brew of guilt, shame, self-judgment, and self-sabotage. You may not even realize that you're being so hard on yourself because you decided to withhold forgiveness.

Counterpunch: Know that it doesn't have to be this way. The way out of this awful trap is to simply love yourself just as you are right now. Put your hand on your heart and with reverence and compassion, say to yourself: "Though I am struggling to let go of this hurt, I fully love and accept myself just as I am." This radical self-acceptance will begin the healing journey of learning to let go of hurts that may have been lodged in your soul for many years.

Jeremiah 29:11: [11] *For I know the thoughts that I think toward you, saith the Lord, thoughts of peace, and not of evil, to give you an expected end.*

7. You're keeping a list of offenses. It's not like you're keeping an actual physical list of all the times you were slighted or offended.... right? Most likely it's a mental list. Each time your offender looks at you the wrong way, or says something offensive, or just ignores you, you catalog the action as part of a long list of offenses you use to justify keeping them trapped in your dungeon. But as you saw above, you may think they're the ones in your dungeon but if you look more closely, you'll see that you're the one inside the prison bars, not outside.

Counterpunch: If your list is so long that you've forgotten the original offense that started you down this dark path, it's probably time to ditch the list. If you already have a written list, you're already halfway there. Just put it in the shredder. If it's in your head, go ahead and write it down then destroy it.

1 Corinthians 13: 13 *Though I speak with the tongues of men and of angels, and have not charity, I am become as sounding brass, or a tinkling cymbal.² And though I have the gift of prophecy, and understand all mysteries, and all knowledge; and though I have all faith, so that I could remove mountains, and have not charity, I am nothing. ³ And though I bestow all my goods to feed the poor, and though I give my body to be burned, and have not charity, it profiteth me nothing. ⁴ Charity suffereth long, and is kind; charity envieth not; charity vaunteth not itself, is not puffed up, ⁵ Doth not behave itself unseemly, seeketh not her own, is not easily provoked, thinketh no evil;*

8. You're sick. That's right. Withholding forgiveness may actually be making you sick. If you're struggling with stress related illness such as anxiety, depression, or high blood pressure, it may be time to try some forgiveness therapy.

Counterpunch: Letting go of bitterness has been said to not only improve the above conditions, but also improve your immune system, heart, and overall mental health. If you're holding on to unforgiveness for dear life, consider the sobering idea that holding on might be slowly taking your life.

Jeremiah 17:14: Heal me, O Lord, and I shall be healed; save me, and I shall be saved: for thou art my praise.

9. You're not taking responsibility for your feelings. Find yourself blaming the person you cannot forgive for your feelings? Maybe you're blaming the weather, or even random events. Understand that when you choose to withhold forgiveness, what you're saying to the offender is: "I hold you responsible not just for what you did to me, but how I reacted and responded to what you did. I hold you responsible for my unhappiness."

Counterpunch: You may be slow to acknowledge it, but this is often the hidden script operating in your heart and soul. But it's a lie, plain and simple. Only you are responsible for your reactions and feelings. By giving that responsibility away to your offender, you're allowing them to have power over you that's not theirs to have.

Unearth the script by saying it to yourself out loud. Write it down. You'll almost immediately recognize and acknowledge the lie in your script. Choose to take back what is rightfully yours—your own reactions and feelings, no matter how unpleasant. This will be key to freeing you from your self-imposed prison.

James 4:17: [17] *Therefore to him that knoweth to do good, and doeth it not, to him it is sin.*

10. You replay the scene over and over...and over. If you find yourself lying awake in bed at 2 a.m. replaying events that happened weeks, months, or years ago, this one may resonate with you. And you know that with each replay, your feelings of being stuck and resentment grows. Sometimes, you find yourself fixating so much on the past that you've allowed it to define everything you do. For instance, if your heart was broken in a past relationship, you may have consciously decided to let people in only so far, even someone you may have grown to love deeply.

Counterpunch: To address this problem try meditation (give yourself 10-20 minutes): Begin noticing your breath and allow yourself to relax for a few minutes. Notice all the feelings that are arising within you as you relax, welcoming both pleasant and unpleasant sensations. Once you've reached a state of deeper relaxation, bring to mind the scene you have been replaying over and over. As you replay the scene, imagine an ending you would have preferred. For instance, if you regret reacting in anger to an offensive remark, imagine yourself responding to the person and yourself with compassion. Imagine yourself in a future encounter with the person or another person. Imagine yourself responding to a similar situation with greater compassion. Rest in these images before slowly bringing yourself out of meditation by gently bringing your awareness back to your body in this space and time. Resolve to begin practicing this in your everyday life. Choose to be responsive rather than reactive going forward.

1 John 4:18: *18 There is no fear in love; but perfect love casteth out fear: because fear hath torment. He that feareth is not made perfect in love.*

11. You gossip about them. It's natural to want to return the hurt to those who have hurt us. One of the primary ways we do this is through gossip. We may divulge their secrets or spread untruths about them behind their backs. If you intend to cause harm with the tongue, you'd be wise to heed the proverb: "Death and life are in the power of the tongue, and those who love it will eat its fruits" (Prov 18:21), When you gossip, you're not only doing further harm to your broken relationship (it's funny how much you say behind a person's back can get back to them), but you also endanger your relationships with the very people you gossip with. While your gossiping may start off as a bonding experience, sooner or later people will learn that you cannot be trusted to hold their confidence. Soon enough, you'll have fewer people of whom you can gossip and even fewer real friends.

Counterpunch: When tempted to say something unkind about your offender, say something you genuinely admire about them. If there is nothing you admire, refrain from speaking.

Ephesians 4:29: *29 Let no corrupt communication proceed out of your mouth, but that which is good to the use of edifying, that it may minister grace unto the hearers.*

12. You refuse to confide in others. We live in a culture that believes that reaching out for help is a sign of weakness. In fact, you may be withholding forgiveness because you believe it might cause you to appear weak in the eyes of others. But if you're reeling from hurt, it may be helpful to share your feelings with a trusted friend—in a non-gossipy way of course. The difference here is that when you gossip, you focus on the actions of the offender instead of focusing on your own feelings and owning them. Just sharing your feelings can provide relief and perspective. It may free you from the stuck feeling and promote creative thinking to help you move on from the hurt and resentment.

Counterpunch: Identify two or three people you could confide in and reach out to one of them today. Don't think about, don't second-guess the people you thought of. Just reach out. Don't let unforgiveness destroy you. Are you ready to let go of past hurts so you can move on with your life? Then it's time to begin letting go of unforgiveness. Know that learning to forgive is a lifelong process. Just like love, forgiveness is a decision we make each day.

Ephesians 4:29: *[29] Let no corrupt communication proceed out of your mouth, but that which is good to the use of edifying, that it may minister grace unto the hearers.*

Forgiveness doesn't mean you have to make amends with who hurt you. It doesn't mean befriending them, sympathizing with them, or validating what they have done to you. It just means accepting that they've left a mark on you. And that for better or for worse, that mark is now your burden to bear. It means you're done waiting for the person who broke you to come put you back together. It's the decision to heal your own wounds, regardless of which marks they're going to leave on your skin. It's the decision to move forward with scars.

Forgiveness isn't about letting injustice reign. It's about creating your own justice, your own karma, and your own destiny. It's about getting back onto your feet and deciding that the rest of your life isn't going to be miserable because of what happened to you. It means walking bravely into the future, with every scar and callous you've incurred along the way. Forgiveness means saying that you're not going to let what happened to you define you any longer. Forgiveness doesn't mean that you are giving up all your power. Forgiveness means you're finally ready to take it back.

CHAPTER THREE

The Foundation of Forgiving

Just as most other behaviors in life, forgiveness or the lack thereof is often rooted in our childhood. Was forgiveness a part of your family and social culture as a child? Did you witness your parents exercise forgiveness to others in the family or community? Did your parents show forgiveness to one another, or did they use past wounds as weapons whenever new arguments occurred? The truth is that it's time for you to take an honest look at the foundation of your ability to forgive and make the needed adjustments if any when it comes to your children.

Many of us grew up hearing family members discussing old grudges towards other family members. Maybe you couldn't play with your first cousins because Aunty Sally had offended your mom years prior and perhaps your mom even felt you were being disloyal by even wanting to fraternize with those she had not forgiven. Perhaps you grew up with severe unforgiveness among your parents who were no longer together. Most parents teach their children to forgive other children, but they tend to want their kids to harbor the same resentments towards adults that they have.

Teaching Children to Forgive

Young children are often taught that the proclamation of "I am sorry" followed by the automatic reply of "I forgive you" can solve any conflict. This may be because we as parents and educators seek a quick solution to interpersonal disputes—and when problems are short-lived, these kinds of quick exchanges help. At the same time, if there is deeper hurt with deeper anger, children need more time to process the unfairness and to feel angry for a while.

To support children's maturing understanding of forgiveness, parents can start by having age-appropriate discussions about it with their kids, based on where kids are in their cognitive and emotional development. These conversations can change the way children think about forgiveness and help them emotionally recover when they inevitably experience harm and unfair treatment from others in life. When kids are wronged and don't forgive, they remain "stuck" in the traumatic situation when they felt victimized. Every time they recall the hurtful event, they re-experience their stress response. If they dwell on their resentment, they continue to release stress chemicals, such as adrenaline, cortisol, and norepinephrine into their brains. This activates the amygdala and other primitive brain regions involved in survival emotions such as fear and rage. The result is an inhibition of the brain's problem-solving ability, creativity, reasoning, and impulse control. Children who learn how to forgive also gain an edge academically, and the reason may be as simple as having more energy available to focus on constructive pursuits. Their brains aren't fuming, recounting the hurt, and plotting revenge; instead, they've got a clean slate where they can organize information and think creatively.

If parents are opposed to forgiving, then at this stage it becomes more difficult for adolescents to learn to appreciate it. Still, if peers and teachers value the norm of forgiving, this can challenge adolescents to think more deeply about it. We get conflicting messages all the time in society, and this is why some of the important groups in an adolescent's life (including families, social media groups, or houses of worship, if they belong to one) might consider talking about the theme of forgiveness as a possible response to unfairness. Adolescents can easily handle the cognitive complexity of holding both forgiveness and justice in mind at the same time: Forgive and seek justice. At its highest developmental level, forgiveness means to unconditionally offer mercy to someone who acted unfairly. College students and adults begin to see that if forgiving is a strong moral virtue, then it should be offered regardless of external factors like punishment, compensation, or the norms of different groups. They tend to see forgiveness as worthy of their time because it is good for families, communities, and entire societies.

When kids are young, forgiveness seems to come naturally. They squabble with siblings or with parents — conflicts that often result in tears and timeouts. But memories of the incident quickly fade. Children are dependent on the love of family, and they're wired to forgive and forget to preserve those relationships. We tell them to apologize to each other, and we apologize to them when appropriate. "It's OK!" kids may respond, before running back to whatever activity had occupied their attention.

Yet we all live in a world broken by sin, and as our children grow, they start having longer memories — holding little grudges, giving more significance to the poor decisions of others. If they don't forgive and can't ask for forgiveness, these relationships suffer and may eventually fall apart. Forgiveness is essential in maintaining any relationship.

It's also the foundation of our faith. We have all sinned and fallen short of God's glory. We all depend on His forgiveness. Remind your kids that God is the perfect model of forgiveness, demonstrated in the words and life of Jesus Christ. There is no greater picture of forgiveness than Jesus — who was mocked, unjustly condemned, beaten, humiliated and nailed to a cross — and still said, "Father, forgive them, for they know not what they do" (Luke 23:34).

I used to tell my children to replace the "them" in Jesus' statement with their own name. They knew, of course, that they didn't take part in Christ's crucifixion, but to approach a deeper understanding of true forgiveness, every child must recognize how his or her sins are the reason Jesus had to suffer. God's grace is the greatest motivator — and the greatest guide — for forgiveness in human relationships. When we truly recognize God's forgiveness of our sins, we are naturally compelled to forgive others (Colossians 3:13). 'It's not fair!'

From our youngest years, most of us have a deep understanding of what we perceive to be fair. (Try giving a Popsicle to one child and not another.) This internal sense of fairness affects our response to offenses against us. We may not say it aloud, but our feeling is something like: *If someone hurts us, shouldn't we hurt them?* It's difficult to be a good forgiver when we want to retaliate.

Teach your kids that true forgiveness is incompatible with our sense of fairness. When we forgive, we relinquish the right and the need to get even. We release the anger we feel toward someone else, recognizing that God will handle the matter in His own way. And His ways are not driven by the human sense of fairness. Indeed, the ultimate "unfairness" was when Jesus endured the punishment for our transgressions against Him. Forgiveness is our freedom. When we release the hurt and the anger, it is our own burden that we drop, our own barrier we demolish. Relationships move forward. Friendships deepen.

God's ultimate act of forgiveness may compel us to forgive others. But forgiveness is an attitude, not an action, and it's never easy. Help them adjust expectations. We often bring rules into a relationship — unspoken rules for how others should behave. I tell my kids that it's better to have preferences and not let those preferences stand in the way of the relationship itself.

Yes, we can encourage friends to do good, but in the end, we simply can't control how others act. We don't know how life has uniquely shaped their decision-making. But we can still accept them and love them, building relationships that aren't steered by our expectations.

Encourage them to see the perspective of others. When we're hurt or betrayed, our pain can often cloud our perspective. As you talk with your children about these moments, help them try to see events from the standpoint of the other person: "Do you think your teammate is acting out in hurtful ways because of some painful times in his own life? Is your friend under a lot of stress with all she's dealing with at school?" Trying to see another person's perspective can make a big difference in helping to forgive him or her. Explain that true forgiveness isn't conditional. Help your kids see that there are two likely outcomes when we forgive someone. Often, it results in building a new, better relationship. But it's also important to recognize that extending forgiveness doesn't depend on any actions from the person they are forgiving. If others continue to reject us, God still commands us to forgive (Matthew 18:21-22).

Indeed, not all forgiveness ends in friendship. I told my kids that just because you forgive someone doesn't mean you need to be friends with him or her. It's wise to recognize when a friendship isn't good for you and to let go of that friendship without feeling any bitterness or anger.

We need not worry about how our forgiveness is received. Whether we get the benefit of a renewed relationship or not, forgiveness is still good for us. Letting go of angry feelings — and moving on with life in a positive way — lifts a huge burden from our shoulders.

Forgiveness may not feel fair. But it is more than fair — it's *freeing*.

The Apologetic Parent

Would you rather ask your child for forgiveness when you've messed up or eat a piece of pizza out of a trash can at a public park? Neither seems pleasant at the time. One of these however does have short term as well as eternal benefits. Jacob reminds us why apologizing is well worth the effort.

1 John 1:9: *If we confess our sins, he is faithful and just and will forgive us our sins and purify us from all unrighteousness.*

Some say they would rather ask for forgiveness than for permission. When it comes down to it, however, it seems that most people opt out of asking for either one! Children, being human and all, probably lean toward the same behavior. Show your children how to ask for forgiveness.

Let's talk about the value in kids experiencing parents asking forgiveness from others and from the kids when the parent has done wrong. A foundation for humility. When a child watches a parent apologize for doing wrong their foundation for humility is strengthened significantly. Someone who grew up watching humble parents will be more likely to accept responsibility when they have done wrong. The child's perception of themselves can be formed around the understanding that they, like their parents, are flawed and that there is a productive way to handle situations when those flaws are revealed. This biblical worldview of self can effectively be established when parents show their kids firsthand what repentance from sin looks like.

They see Jesus in you instead of just seeing you. This should be every Christian parent's greatest aspiration—to show their child Jesus! God's word teaches Jesus showing His power in the midst of human weakness. Seeking forgiveness from others is one of the most practical ways to let this process take place. Children who have forgiveness-seeking parents get a front row seat to the glory of Jesus Himself, for true humility only comes from Him. What greater joy can a parent have than to know their humility encourages their children to love Jesus more? Your relationship will grow. To ask forgiveness is to ask for healing in a hurting relationship. Whatever wound the victim may have received begins to heal and trust begins to grow. Genuine reconciliation is only possible with the forgiveness of sin. This is the reason mankind and God can be in relationship in the first place! Due to God's initiation of forgiveness, parents can experience the same reconciling power with their children upon asking forgiveness.

Owning our sin and asking for forgiveness is hard! Especially when it is our own child we have hurt. This is a great practice, however, to raise a child who sees Jesus clearly, who is humble, and who loves their mom and dad more because of their exemplified humility.

The Mama Trauma: Forgiving Your Mother

Mothers mold us — often physically in the womb (though there are many other types of mother-child relationships, including adoptive ones) and emotionally through their interactions with us.

The bond is so strong that there's no such thing as an infant, but only an infant and their mother. He believed that a child's sense of self is built by the kind of a relationship that they have with their primary caregiver (usually mom).

So, what happens if mom wasn't there for you emotionally? That's usually when people experience The Mama Trauma.

Who typically experiences The Mama Trauma?

Children (usually daughters, but sometimes also sons) are said to experience the mama trauma if their mother:

- provided support by taking care of the physical needs of the children, but didn't give love, care, and security
- didn't provide empathy to mirror the child's emotions and help them label and manage those emotions
- didn't allow the child to express negative emotions
- was extra critical

- expected the child's support with their own physical or emotional needs
- wasn't available to the child either because they had to work or because they were busy with their own interests (Do note, however: You can be a working mom — even a working single mom — *without* instilling the mother wound!)
- had suffered emotional or physical abuse themselves, didn't process the trauma, and was therefore unable to offer love and nurture
- had an untreated mental health condition
- experienced alcoholism or drug addiction

Daughters and sons can both experience the mama trauma

The mother wound is not a specific diagnosis — although it can hurt so much that you're sure it warrants one. While both daughters and sons can feel the impact of the under-mothering that leads to the mother wound, it's typically considered a mother-to-daughter wound.

We all know that the trust that a mother instills in childhood positively affects not only the child's present, but also their future relationships. Meaning, a child who acquires the mother wound is most likely to perpetuate this type of relationship with their own children.

In patriarchal societies, it may be easier for mothers to pass on their own mama trauma to their daughters. Women who have internalized stereotypical beliefs that relegate women to second-class citizens are more likely to consciously or unconsciously transmit these beliefs to their daughters.

Daughters in these societies may find themselves caught in a double-edged dilemma: Accept what Mom believes in so that we're in the same boat and she keeps on loving me, or fight for my own beliefs and aim for empowerment.

What are the signs and effects of the mama trauma?

If you're wondering which signs could signal the presence of the mama trauma in your life, think back to your childhood, and try to recall what the child version of you experienced.

If many of the feelings in the list below seem familiar, you may have a mama trauma:

- Your mother just wasn't there for you on an emotional level.
- You were reluctant to turn to your mother for comfort or security.
- You doubted you had your mother's approval, so you were always trying to be perfect.
- You felt nervous and frightened around your mother.
- Your mother expected you to take care of her physically or emotionally.

If the points on the list above resonate with you, what does that mean for you now? These negative feelings can lead to:

- low self-esteem
- lack of emotional awareness
- inability to self-soothe
- the feeling that warm and nurturing relationships aren't in your reach

Let's see why this could happen:

Low self-esteem

Secure attachment makes a child feel that they matter. Without this basic belief in themselves, children struggle to get a sense of self and to believe in themselves.

Lack of emotional awareness

A mother who is present for their child can mirror their child's feelings, label those feelings, and help them to manage the feelings. The child doesn't need to suppress negative feelings because they have a way to manage them.

Inability to self-soothe

Without the awareness of how to manage their feelings, children and later adults never develop the ability to self-soothe. Instead, they turn to things outside of themselves for comfort. These things could include numbing activities like alcohol and drugs.

Relationship difficulties

Adults with the mother wound have difficulty forming and maintaining the positive relationships that we all crave for because they've never learned to trust.

Steps for healing from the mama trauma

Healing from the mama trauma is a balance between acknowledging negative feelings such as anger and resentment and recognizing that we may need to forgive our mother. While remaining mired in the negative feelings may make us feel temporarily right, in the long run, we lose out.

So how do we get the balance that will heal us?

Express the pain

The first step is letting yourself say, "Ouch" — and more — if you need to. Therapy can help your child-self express the pain of being unloved, ignored, shunned, ridiculed, and even victimized. Journaling can also help.

Love yourself

Our concept of self was built through the way our mother interacted with us. We need to realize that the fact that our mother was unable to build our self-image in a positive way was not our fault. By letting go of the less-than-ideal image, we can recreate our self-image.

Develop self-awareness

Without our mother's feedback, we didn't have the reinforcement needed to develop self-awareness. We need to learn how to get in touch with our emotions. Take the time to stop and feel what you're feeling. Naming the feeling is the first step to coping with the feeling.

Parent yourself

We can also learn how to parent ourselves and give ourselves all the things we never received as a child. Self-care isn't spoiling ourselves; it's taking care of our needs. For some of us, self-care is a solo morning walk before settling down at your desk. For others, it's taking time off for a coffee date with a friend who makes us feel good about ourselves.

Forgiveness

Acknowledging our own feelings and grieving over what we never got as a child creates the emotional space needed to move towards forgiveness.

Mothering is hard work. If you're a mother, you already know that. And sometimes mothers get things wrong. Even very wrong. If you can recognize your mother for who she is and not dwell on who you'd like her to be, you can move toward understanding her and accepting her.

Once you've done that, it could be possible to build a relationship with your mother. Learn to set boundaries and you may find that together you and your mother can build some sort of relationship. Even if it's not the perfect relationship, it can become something meaningful.

Of course, in some cases, you may have had a neglectful or abusive mother that you truly cannot forgive. In such cases, it may be better to work through those hard feelings within your support network or with a therapist — without extending the olive branch.

It would be convenient and easy if we could blame all of our faults and failures on our mothers. But it wouldn't be truthful. And that's because we all have the gift of choice.

We can choose to take the steps to heal our own mama trauma and to make sure that we don't pass on this hurt to our children.

The Father Fracture: Finally Forgiving the Father

Fathers play such a vital and important role in the development of a child. The effects of an emotionally or physically absent father can impact an individual's self-esteem, relationships and even their motivation in life. A father fracture can instill feelings of not meeting expectations, not being good enough and being undeserving of love. Children don't have the insight to understand that their parents can have problems, so they tend to internalize their parents' behavior as their fault. Low self-esteem can result in an individual:

- Never pushing themselves in school or work
- Having difficulty opening up and connecting with others, making it hard to form meaningful, long-lasting relationships and friendships
- Being more susceptible to substance abuse

A father fracture can leave a person feeling low, depressed, or anxious about their parental relationship. A parent is supposed to offer unconditional love, and if you see that others have that, it's hard to understand why you don't. Often, this anxiety or depression turns to anger. Individuals may feel robbed of a happy, normal childhood. They may also feel deeply hurt by their father's actions or absenteeism and grow resentful.

If your father often arrived late or missed important events in your life, you may overcompensate by setting extremely rigid boundaries in adulthood. You may feel everything needs to be scheduled and planned, and you can't easily forgive people for being late, canceling or wanting to reschedule. This is an attempt to regain a sense of control you didn't have growing up with an absent father.

Another possibility is the other extreme of having loose boundaries. If your father was overly critical and never seemed happy with what you did, you may develop the need to please people. You desperately want acceptance and approval, so you're unable to say no. If certain people in your life notice this behavior, they may be quick to take advantage of it.

Your parents are your first example of what a relationship looks like. Most people unconsciously seek to replicate the relationship dynamic with their parents in their relationships in adulthood. Without your realizing it, a father fracture may cause you to seek partners who repeat the negative behaviors of your father. This can mean a partner who's absent, overbearing or overly critical. We seek this out because it brings a sense of familiarity and comfort. However, choosing a partner similar to your father only repeats your trauma from childhood.

Unfortunately, victims of abuse can sometimes continue the cycle when they become parents themselves. If you didn't have a solid example of good parenting, it's harder to be a good parent yourself. You might find yourself unwittingly repeating the mistakes your father made. Of course, if someone has endured pain, they want to protect their child from going through the same experience. This makes addressing your father fracture is critical not just for you, but for your partner(s) and your children.

You may have a father fracture if you can identify key indicators when reflecting on your childhood. These can include that your father:

- Was frequently absent
- Was emotionally absent or abusive

- Was highly critical of you and constantly disapproved of your actions, choices, and behaviors
- Withheld food, love, or other essentials as a form of punishment
- Was physically abusive

You may also recall that you often felt scared of your father or feel your relationship was never good and remains rocky or nonexistent today. Below are steps on how to finally heal the Father Fracture.

- Accept that your father is a child of God
- Accept that your father did what he had the mental and spiritual capacity to do.
- Forgive your father for not knowing what he did not know
- Accept that your father is just as flawed of a human as you are.
- Accept who your father is/was instead of who you desired him to be. This doesn't mean that you can necessarily maintain a new relationship with him, but you will be able to remove the longing expectancy for him to be someone else.

CHAPTER FOUR

Misconceptions of Forgiveness

Let's discuss some misconceptions surrounding forgiveness that prevent people from using it. These come not only from misunderstandings but also the reactive anger of our fight-and-flight reactions. The choice is whether to use the highest brain functions (where forgiveness comes from) or use the more primitive brain areas where anger and resentment lie.

Recognizing the following misconceptions can help you to become willing to forgive, which is the first step in forgiving. Each one of these misconceptions can cause years of suffering for a person. These are not listed in an order of importance.

I cannot forgive because they keep doing it!

This is probably the hardest of all the misconceptions to get through. If a person continues to hurt your feelings intentionally or even unintentionally, out of habit, or because they do not know any better, forgiveness can still be beneficial, although, admittedly, it is more difficult. Even though someone continues to commit the offense, forgiveness can still occur because forgiving wipes away the hurts of the past – even if it was only 15 minutes before.

Putting the offense out of sight, out of mind, or forgetting about it may not always be forgiveness. It can be the denial of the effects of the offending act. Forgiveness acknowledges what was done and chooses to let it go, but not by avoiding its impact. Avoiding the impact just keeps the negative effects below the surface of the mind.

I'm just too angry! (or too hurt!)

It is essential in forgiving to be aware of your feelings. You can see the effects of too much emotion in the violence caused by anger. Each time you bring up anger and hostility your whole physiology goes into stress, which continues to activate the reactive brains. Yes, forgiveness has its timing. But I've found that whenever people decide to deal with the hurt or anger with forgiving, they move through it more quickly.

Before I forgive, I need an apology!

You may wait forever and not get the admission of guilt you want. The person who caused the upset may have a different perspective of what happened and feel that an apology is unnecessary. In fact, he or she might be expecting an apology from you! By forgiving, you will regain your own happiness and peace of mind, and not be dependent on someone else's actions. You will stop becoming the victim. Even if they do give an apology, it may not be heartfelt if it comes at your insistence. Forgive without the apology and save yourself time, energy, and heartache.

If I forgive, I will be condoning or justifying their offense.

Forgiveness is not condoning bad behavior or justifying an offense. We think that if we condone, we think the offense is acceptable and thus, forgiveness is not necessary. Forgiveness is needed when we are hurt and grieving in some way about how we were mistreated. The family of a drug abuser may forgive him or her for the behavior but does not approve of the drug misuse and will probably do everything they can to stop the abuse.

They do not deserve it!

You might be right – they might not deserve forgiveness. Nevertheless, you are forgiving for yourself, for your benefit, and for your relationships. I've often seen forgiveness for those who don't deserve it. Who knows whether the forgiven ones were affected, but the people doing the forgiving certainly felt much better?

The person is no longer around, so I don't need to forgive!

You might think, "out of sight, out of mind." But, if you still carry the upsetting emotions and ideas, then the injury remains alive in you. At some level, harboring any resentment, large or small, affects your life and interactions with people. Though forgiveness may be an act of compassion for someone who is gone or deceased, it is mainly to relieve you of the self-inflicted torture of hate and anger.

I don't have to forgive because I never want to see them again!

Forgiveness does not mean reconciliation. Reconciliation, which is the reunion of two upset parties, is not necessarily the outcome of forgiving. A person can forgive and still choose to protect him or herself from abusive behavior by never seeing that person again. Trust must be re-earned. That is what reconciliation is about.

They will just hurt me again if I forgive!

Forgiving does not mean turning the other cheek to allow the offense to occur again. Jesus' original meaning of "turn the other cheek" was to show your strength in your faith. Its broader meaning includes forgiveness but is not limited to it.

When a relationship has reached the point of physical or emotional abuse, it is in deep trouble. Outside help is needed. Limit sitting on the abuse is urgent. Working on a domestically violent relationship requires at least a psychotherapist trained specifically in this area. It is not work you do alone. You must protect yourself. Even emotional abuse needs to be stopped. But if there is no option – and sometimes it seems there isn't – forgiveness can help. But try to get external help too.

There is too much to forgive!

Sometimes, a person, group, or organization is just too difficult to forgive because he, or she or they did so much. Break it down. List all the offenses the person committed and forgive each one.

People will think I am weak to let the other person win.

This is common for men BUT come on! Carrying hate and anger and the physiological problems that follow is winning????

I've tried, but I can't.

There may be many reasons why you can't forgive, but that doesn't mean it can't be done. You are gaining the tools now to successfully forgive. Sometimes a person will forgive and then regret it. That happens because of reactionary brain activity.

I just want to forget about it. or I can't forget about it.

In forgiving, people are not being asked to forget. On the contrary, it is important to remember, so that we should not let such atrocities happen again. Forgiveness does not mean condoning what has been done. It means taking what happened seriously, not minimizing it; drawing out the sting in the memory that threatens our entire existence.

Forgetting about an injury might not be forgiveness but rather, denial. The negative results of this denial impinge insidiously under the surface of your mind. You know you have forgiven when the offender has harmless passage through your mind. Forgiveness allows the upset to fade in the mind because it is no longer run by the upset and can refocus on the positives of life.

Only God Forgives or God will deal with them, so I don't have to.

It's not true that you don't have to do anything, because you will still have the upset there affecting you while you wait for the person's divine punishment. This doesn't relieve you of the upset and doesn't guarantee that God agrees with you.   Though we may speculate on how God might judge someone we cannot possibly know God's perspective of a situation because we are unable to take the 360-degree God's-eye-view of that person or situation.

We cannot see the past, or often, the present situation that made the person decide to do what he or she did. We cannot know all the dynamics involved in their life. We often do not see the forces involved in our own lives that cause us to make a particular decision. Thus, all we can really do is our own work, and let God do God's work. In our own lives, forgiveness is up to us for our own happiness.

The idea only God forgives is not true. People of all lifestyles, religious or not, forgive regularly, much to their benefit and the benefit of others. Those without any religious orientation can enjoy the same positive benefits from letting go of old hatreds and resentments as a religious person. I've worked with atheists and people from many different religions, all of whom have experienced radical changes in their lives through forgiving. Forgiveness is a movement of the mind and heart toward compassion, kindness, and love. It is an act of peace, which results in joy for the forgiver, regardless of religious belief.

These misconceptions and misunderstandings about forgiving keep it from being done. I hope this summary has helped you understand forgiveness and has moved you closer to forgiving. Forgiveness doesn't mean that you're saying that the other person is "right" or that what they did is/was "OK". Forgiveness is about choosing (and re-choosing) to let go so that you don't get stuck living in the past. You forgive, not to anoint the other party with something but to release you to move on and evolve beyond it.

Big blocks around forgiveness are fear of condoning, that we're giving them or the universe the blueprints to screw us over, or that we look "weak". We also fear being vulnerable by putting ourselves out there again and putting ourselves back together. It's like, *What if I forgive and then I try again at life and get screwed over? What if they think that they've gotten away with it?*

It's about getting into the present because when you're actively or passively holding on, you're not letting go. You might be trying to right the wrongs of the past in some way. Or maybe you're 'dining' what may be every single day on the anger and other emotions. You may keep rubbing your face in where you feel that you've erred. Or you might rub your face in the other person's behavior while blaming you for it too.

Forgiving doesn't mean, *I'm right, they're wrong.* or *I'm wrong, they're right.* It's about deciding to be done. Part of our reluctance to let go and forgive is about our relationship with ourselves. Not the outer one that we project but the inner one driven by our thoughts and feelings 'conversations'. It's what goes on behind closed doors.

Many of us are attached to the narrative, to the 'reasoning habits' (beliefs). It often feels easier to keep telling the stories while berating us in the process, or to almost feel righteous about how wrong the other person is. We forget that we're not fully occupying our actual lives. The story of our lives continue but are, until we decide to let go, becoming a story about us telling a story.

If you've struggled with deciding to be done, where are you judging you in some way?

Are you reluctant to let go of the security blanket of the story and your position? You might feel righteous or consumed by the injustice of it all.

Where are you reluctant to trust you and move on?

Where are you holding onto a 'child role' and avoiding responsibility?

CHAPTER FIVE

Why Can't I Forgive?

I think this is a great time to stop and speak on the ability to forgive. I know that it can all be easier said than done. I understand that fully. We have all been told that we not only have the commandment to forgive, but we also possess some supernatural ability to forgive also. I don't know about you, but I can admit that sometimes I didn't feel every supernatural when trying to forgive someone that harmed me. There have been times that I simply didn't want to forgive, and there have been other times in which I really wanted to forgive, but I felt stuck. I felt that something was blocking my ability to tap into my gift of forgiveness and activate it.

Sometimes we experience this because we foolishly think that forgiveness means that the wound will no longer hurt, I won't be upset any longer, or it will be as if it never occurred. That is not forgiving. That is forgetting, or at minimum that is erasing the event from every happening in the beginning. That's not God's will, because there is a lesson in every trial. As appealing as undoing the harm may seem, it will not help you in the greater scheme of your journey with God. So, why can't I forgive even when I want to? Usually, these feelings occur in the most intimate of relationships that have gone off track such as romantic relationships. Often when we desire to forgive our spouse, the bandwidth to do so just doesn't show up. The next few pages I will speak specifically on romantic relationships, but the principles apply to platonic relationships as well.

Relationship Capital

Imagine that your relationship is a bank account and in this bank account is $100.00 that you and your spouse have both deposited into the account. However, the $100.00 is not actually money. Instead, the $100.00 is the value of trust. Now imagine that every time you or your spouse is dishonest or disloyal a withdrawal is made from that account. So, now you're no longer at a $100.00 balance of trust. Now you might only have $65.00. Can you make it with $65.00? That's tricky. However, this is where most people get it wrong. Just because you didn't cost all your trust doesn't mean you still have enough to be careless with. You should immediately take efforts to add funds back into the account of trust because forgiveness is expensive. Sometimes you'll even have to pay interest rates to get your account to a stable standing.

The worst thing you could do is to convince yourself that a relationship that you anticipate will last forever will make it off $65.00 in the fund of trust. Why is that a ridiculous logic? You're human. Your spouse is human. Trust me! This is what happens when your spouse has disproportioned reactions to your mistakes. You may ask yourself, "Why did she blow up like that over such a minor situation?" Well, as minor as the matter may be to you, it may have cost more of the fund of trust.

When you begin losing relationship capital at a steady rate and neither party is making any efforts to rebuild the balance, then disaster is on the way. This is typically the reason behind our struggles to forgive. You may have the desire to forgive. You may have the love to forgive. You just might not have the relationship capital to forgive because someone kept spending and spending your trust on small things so that when mountains arose you had nothing left to cover the cost of it.

Here's the thing. In marriage, we become one. So that means, forgiveness must be a joint effort and both parties have to be willing to do the work on giving and receiving forgiveness. Marriage changes the forgiveness dynamic because of the oneness of the covenant. If a husband has been unfaithful to his wife, then he must be willing to do whatever necessary to replenish the account and heal. The wife must be willing to allow the account to be replenished. It is of great importance that both parties no when the account has been closed. If the relationship capital account keeps a healthy growing balance, then the relationship can continue growing and healing. However, when the cost of forgiveness becomes greater than the balance of the account, the relationship will struggle to survive.

Whether a conflict is minor or earth shattering, forgiveness is an essential part of moving forward. Sometimes, though, we can be too caught up in feeling hurt to think clearly about forgiveness, or simply hold too much anger to want to offer it at all.

Let's take a step back though, and explore what forgiveness means.

Real forgiveness has two parts: letting go and moving forward.

Letting go is a big hurdle on its own, because it means releasing feelings of anger and resentment over a perceived offense. Now, it's important to remember that idea of perception – no matter what the problem at hand might be. You and your spouse will have different versions of what happened, and even if they are totally at fault in your eyes, they might not see it exactly that way. Regardless, letting go of that resentment and anger is the only way to prevent the issue from paralyzing your marriage.

The next step, moving forward, is just as important. It means doing away with any desire for punishment, retribution, or restitution for the wrongdoing. If you still want your spouse to be punished, then you are still harboring resentment.

You have to understand: the past is the past, and it cannot be changed. No matter how angry you are, how hurt you feel… What's done is done. Forgiveness – both letting go and moving forward – is all about the future. You can't change the past, but you can certainly make choices that will influence your future. You keep your marriage "in prison" if you focus on the issues of the past, and you set it free when you let go of problems that have already happened to start focusing on solutions.

Forgiving, however, is a little easier said than done. There are a few major roadblocks that prevent people from getting to a place of forgiveness for their spouse. To overcome them, we first must understand them:

1. Believing Forgiveness Condones Behavior

Just because you forgive your spouse, it doesn't mean that what they did is ok.

You aren't condoning the behavior; you're just making your future a higher priority than holding onto a grudge. Forgiveness is not about saying everything's ok. It's NOT ok. Instead, forgiveness is about understanding how mistakes are made, understanding that you can take responsibility for your future, and deciding that your marriage is something worth fighting for.

2. Scorekeeping

We may do it unconsciously but holding on to resentment is sometimes a way of keeping score. "She hurt me worse" or "he deserves to feel terrible after what he did to me" are just going to keep you and your spouse further apart. Keeping track of (and retaliating for) who hurt who will only bring more trouble. Your marriage can't win if you're keeping score against each other.

3. Different Standards

One of the hardest obstacles to overcome is realizing we may be holding difficult-to-meet standards – or at least, holding our spouses to higher standards than we than we do for ourselves. This can be tough to admit, but if you can realize that we're all just human, that people make mistakes, and that it's unfair (and unwise) to hold people to standards we can't personally meet, forgiveness comes much easier.

4. Expecting A Guarantee

Your spouse can know that what they did was wrong, they can regret it and apologize profusely. They can do everything in their power to prevent the mistake from happening again, but they can't guarantee it. There are NO guarantees here, just the best intentions and your best efforts. Accepting that things can't be perfect, and that you're never 100% certain the problem won't happen again – or that YOU won't make a mistake just as bad – allows you to move past the problem and work on building a marriage where the issues are less likely to happen.

5. Ineffective Apologies

If the apology doesn't seem sincere, it can be very difficult to forgive. Unfortunately, many people who might mean every word of an apology don't actually get their message across successfully. There are several important steps to presenting a sincere apology, and if they are overlooked, the breakdown in communication can make the apology less than effective. If you're having a hard time forgiving, revisit the "apology stage" and go over what went wrong, how you both feel about it, and what can be done to make it better.

6. Lack of Understanding

To forgive your spouse, you will likely want to know how and why the issue happened in the first place. This can involve some tough admissions of your own role in the problems – or at least the climate of your marriage that led to them. It also involves doing some "outside looking in" investigating to see exactly what happened, evaluating how it can be avoided in the future, and looking for changes that can be made to help ensure a better future.

7. Holding On to Power

When your spouse is trying to be forgiven, and it's your choice to accept their apology or not, you're holding all the power. While it might feel like a good dynamic for the relationship – a way for you to see the changes you'd like, a way to punish your spouse's mistakes, etc. – it's actually poison for your marriage, and will only breed more problems and resentment down the road. Healthy marriages are about cooperation and support, not one person holding power over another.

8. Worried about the opinions of others

This is a major roadblock in forgiveness among couples, especially if the transgression was made public. Public humiliation is a deep wound, and while I encourage people to not live their lives focused on the opinions of other people, we have to be honest. None of us like to be embarrassed. However, we can easily become uneasy about the opinions of our friends and family should we forgive our spouse. Here is the thing. If you truly desire for your relationship to work, then you have to focus more on the purpose than the current position. Sometimes you have to focus more on the destination than the current traffic jam.

If you can't find a way to forgive your spouse for their mistakes, large or small, you won't be able to get past the hurt they've caused – and if you're holding on to the pain, you won't be working toward a better, healthier marriage. Learn to forgive so you can create the marriage you deserve. Here are a few statements we've all heard in our relationships or the relationships of those around us that depict inaccurate ideas about forgiveness:

"I just forgive too easily"

We have all have family or friends who proudly defend their poor relationship choices with, "I just forgive too easily." I would like to say that if it was *easy* it probably wasn't forgiveness. Far too often we choose to turn a blind eye to our pain, ignore our wound, and force ourselves to forget what has occurred out of fear of being alone. This is not forgiveness. Forgiveness is an emotionally bloody sport! Forgiveness is a muscle and it's going to cause some pain to strengthen that muscle. Bodybuilders never find it quite easy to lift significant weight. Instead, they stop focusing on what is easy, and focus on the goal.

"If I didn't forgive you, I wouldn't still (fill in the blank)"

Forgiveness leads back to the road of celebration in your relationship. However, many people in relationships never forgave their spouses for hurts caused decades ago, going with the motion is not forgiveness. There is a difference between celebrating your spouse and tolerating your spouse. Sometimes tolerating your spouse is just simply doing the wifely or husbandly duties or expectancies just out of routine. Once forgiveness has truly taken place, you will find yourself not only seeing new reasons to celebrate your spouse but having the emotional stamina to do so!

"I'll forgive once I'm even"

It pities me that I even feel I have to include this statement. However, you'd be surprised of the number of people who think the solution to resolving conflicts within their relationships is to make their partner feel what they feel. We see this behavior often when infidelity has occurred. Let me first say this. Promiscuity is not revenge, it's promiscuity. Infidelity has an uncanny ability to inspire a desire for revenge. Studies confirm what we intuitively know – that sexual unfaithfulness falls under some of the most hurtful experiences. Many betrayed spouses contemplate having an affair of their own to get even or make themselves feel better. Being scorned and wanting retribution is an expected response to betrayal.

Finding out about sexual and emotional infidelity can lead to broken hearts and relationships coming to an abrupt and painful end; as well as abandonment, intimate partner violence, and loss of resources when these resources are invested into affair partners, and a person might act rashly in their attempts to decrease the pain.

However, revenge on a cheater is not the way to go, and there are many significant reasons why. When you feel shattered and betrayed, revenge after infidelity seems acceptable. Acting out of anger and hurt doesn't make you the best decision-maker. Hence, when you get some space, and things cool down, you might want to take your actions back. Therefore, if you consider revenge after being cheated on, at least give yourself time before you act on it. Give a deadline until which you must remain faithful.

Hopefully, by then, you will have considered all the consequences, and cheating payback is no longer your choice. Cheating to get even with a spouse could make you more like your spouse than you would want in your and other's eyes. They hurt you with infidelity, and now you are cheating back as revenge. How will you feel knowing you did (almost) the same thing as them? Will it give you a new outlook on what they did, and will you feel pressured to forgive them?

If you are looking to make yourself feel better, this is not the right approach. Revenge for cheating won't get you the peace you are looking for. It won't decrease the hurt; rather, it will only pile on more anger and bitterness that you must deal with. Another reason to avoid revenge cheating is to prevent your partner from using your actions to get off the hook. Your revenge cheating can be used as an argument to prove fidelity is difficult and that infidelity happens easily. They might say, "now you know how easy it is to slip up" or "now that you have done it too, you must forgive me." Revenge adultery helps the person who betrayed you to feel less guilty for their actions and ask for more understanding.

The best revenge for cheaters is to show them they chose the easy way out in search of happiness and demonstrate the willpower to avoid doing the same thing. Perhaps you are wondering, "Should I have an affair to show them how much it hurts?" If what you are looking for is to decrease the pain, cheating on a cheater is not the right path. Revenge of any kind rarely holds the key to the peace you so eagerly want. Revenge cheating will most likely, only for a short while, help you feel less pain, but it will pile on another thing to get over in the long run. Revenge cheating won't be of any help in dealing with the feelings or making a plan for overcoming the situation.

It only seems as though getting revenge on a cheating spouse will make things even and better, but unfortunately, it won't. The only way to deal with it is to go through it. Getting revenge on a cheater deteriorates chances of a marriage surviving the infidelities. If you think there is a way you could make it work, restrict yourself from cheating revenge. This spiral will pull you both down.

If you can't stand them anymore, it is better to end it right away. Trying to get the relationship back on track by going this far sounds like trouble. Revenge cheating won't make you even and allow you to start over. To give reconciliation a chance, you need to address the root cause of problems. Furthermore, healing and forgiving infidelity are facilitated by hearing a sincere apology from the cheating spouse. Revenge cheating will only mask the root problems and hearing the other's sincere regret.

People considering this option might feel revenge after infidelity will bring their confidence back. Yet it will do the opposite. When you have an affair of your own, you might feel more desired and attractive for a short period. It can help you see that there are other fish in the sea and know you have options. For a moment, you will renew the sense of self-worth and feel a slight relief. However, other feelings will soon creep in. At that moment, the confidence you acquired will deflate, and all the feelings you tried to avoid will come rushing back.

If you have been betrayed, you might be wondering, "should I cheat on my wife or should I cheat on my husband." Regardless of the reason you are considering it, you should know revenge cheating won't take away the pain or make things better. There are many reasons to avoid revenge on a cheating partner. Revenge on a cheater is supposed to hurt them, but somehow you end up being additionally hurt. Furthermore, when things cool down, you will look back on revenge cheating and see yourself differently. You might want to take your actions back, but you won't be able to.

Bible verses about forgiveness help in viewing the other person as a human being requiring grace and not scolding. Apart from that, it also allows God to forgive your sins. The book of Matthew 6:14-15 says, "If you forgive others their trespasses, your heavenly Father will also forgive you, but if you do not forgive others their trespasses, neither will your Father forgive your trespasses." Forgiveness allows for mediation between man and God. Once someone sins against the other, sin opens up their mind, and they realize they have sinned against the other person, as was the case with Adam and Eve in the Garden of Eden.

Adam realized he had sinned once he bit that fruit. What this did was he felt some sense of shame, and for the first time, he realized he was naked. Adam immediately seeks God.

Asking for forgiveness tames you down, and you want to ask for forgiveness. Even in marriages, couples who go that route understand what comes along with sinning. Forgiveness will bring you back to God. Just like it did to Adam and Eve after God graciously forgave them as in Genesis 3:15. It is against the will of God for marriages to end up in divorces, as in Matthew 19:8.

Why do divorces happen? Simply because couples are not ready to forgive each other! The reason being, they have forgotten how forgiveness feels and the repercussions of forgiveness—given a chance, forgiveness breeds redemption among people, just as John 3:16 tells us. Thus, as per the Bible verses about forgiveness, a marriage can flourish if you are able to forgive your spouse from your heart. If you are able to do that, you can free yourself from the misery of suffering more than your spouse.

CHAPTER SIX

Inner forgiveness

Forgiving self is a battle, a war, an all-out brawl of one's emotional and spiritual mind. If we are honest, our struggles to forgive others is generally linked to our struggles to forgive ourselves. But isn't that what it all keeps boiling down to, self? Everything comes back to self. So, the quality of your life with man and life with God is really all based upon your relationship with self. You will never have the ability to give what you do not have, and it is only when you have an abundance of forgiveness that you offer to yourself that you have some left over to offer to others. People who never seem to forgive others and are always angry at someone are people who are always angry with themselves. They cannot give what they do not possess.

Forgiveness is never easy. But forgiving yourself can be the most challenging type of forgiveness out there. Like it or not, self-forgiveness takes work that requires both compassion and empathy. If you have struggled with believing you are a bad person, coping with guilty feelings, wondering how to make amends, and awareness of your flaws, try to go easy on yourself. There's always a next time, and while your remorse is likely normal, the best gift you can give yourself is to put the past in the past and try to move on.

Self-hatred, guilt, and shame are monsters. Guilt is the emotion we feel following a mistake we've made. Shame is the feeling that our entire life or existence is a mistake. There is a significant difference between guilt and shame, and if we are not careful, those to monsters will quickly introduce us to their uncle, self-hatred. Self-hatred occurs when we no longer possess the skills or ability to regulate our feelings of shame or guilt. So then, we hate ourselves.

If God is love, and love is God then self-hatred with the unconscious withholding of oneself from God. God and hatred cannot occupy the same space so as long as we swim in a river of self-hatred, we disconnect ourselves from God. Now we all know people who seem as if they never feel any sense of shame or guilt. We'd love to see them hold their heads down in shame of their poor behaviors or treatments of others. However, that's not our place. It is never our place to measure one's series of self-loathing.

Forgiveness of yourself or others is hard. But with yourself, it can be even harder as an inner critic and guilt will work against you. To begin the work of forgiving yourself, you must first understand what self-forgiveness means. Self-forgiveness is the cognitive ability to separate an act from a person. An example of this would be having an affair. In this example, while what you have done is adultery or infidelity, it is separate from who you are as a person. While the act itself was wrong, it does not have to define who you are. People make mistakes and the best we can do is make amends and try our best not to repeat them. No human being is perfect. Self-forgiveness is understanding this and being okay with past wrongs. The great news about self-forgiveness is that when you practice on yourself, it will be easier to forgive other people too.

Forgiveness can be a challenge that takes both a lot of work and time to pass. When worried about how long it will take to forgive yourself, it is essential to remember why forgiveness is important in the first place. The following is a list of symptoms you or someone you know may be experiencing due to the inability to forgive yourself:

- Sleeping issues
- Anger
- Resentment
- Difficulty enjoying activities

- Depression, clinical or otherwise

- Repeat behaviors and offenses to escape the guilt of the initial offense

- Escalating behavior and relationship challenges

- Trouble in primary relationships

- Issues at home or work

- Problems with physical health due to the additional stress of carrying guilt

If you wonder why it is important to forgive yourself, the list above should help you out. Whatever you have done, ask yourself, is it really worth all those challenges when you can instead put your time and energy into forgiving yourself? There are acute dangers of holding onto anger, guilt, self-hate, and negativity. Guilt, for example, is one of the most powerful emotions out there. It can spiral you into a cycle of self-abuse and damage your overall self-esteem. Being stuck in negative feelings can also impact your decision-making, cause you to sabotage yourself in relationships both personal and career.

Do you ever find that it's hard for you to forgive yourself and you will always blame yourself? You never appreciate your hard work, and you always feel that your efforts will never be enough to make other people accept you. You care too much about other people's approval and put that weight on your own shoulders. Even your surroundings will make you unhappy. When you hate everything about yourself, you will hate the world you live in too. Thus, you will always find negativity more often than the positivity; you don't like your society, your lifestyle, your environment, even the air. You're actually trying to escape from yourself, not the place where you live.

When you love yourself enough, no matter how cruel the world is, you will never have the feeling of wanting to run away from reality because you are your home. As cliché as it is, please remember that if you can't love yourself enough, who will?

Many of us wrestle everyday with feelings of self-hatred and we have convinced ourselves that our unhealthy behaviors are everything other than an inability to forgive ourselves for not being *perfect*. We all know that self-hate is easier to do than self-love. Little do you know; your everyday behavior could show whether you love yourself or vice versa. Here are 8 signs that actually you hate yourself and you need to change immediately.

1. You're being obsessed with social media.

When you hate yourself, you will always need approval and validation from others. If you constantly check your social media accounts just to find out how many likes you get or how many people view your Insta story, you need to pause and ask yourself why. Realize that you don't need people to like your post if you like yourself enough in real life.

2. You have trouble accepting compliments.

It's hard for you to believe that you are at all worthy of compliments. Thus, no matter how many people give you compliments, you won't believe them. When they give you compliments, you insecurely question them and feel like they don't mean it. You're too self-critical and it kills your self-esteem.

3. You always put extra effort towards fit in.

When you hate being yourself, you will try so hard to be somebody else that you will almost always fake it around others, and your life is all about building a good impression. When you love yourself enough, you won't even care about impressions. You'll practice self-love by doing whatever you love to do, and you will surround yourself with the people who are genuinely accepting of you.

4. You take other people's criticisms personally.

You don't believe in compliments, but you take other people's critiques too seriously. For you, their opinions about your life are extremely important, because you always see your success through other people's eyes. You care too much about what people say. You always let other people control your thoughts because it's hard for you to realize that this is your life, not theirs.

5. You compare yourself to others.

For you, the grass is always greener on the other side. You don't get the concept of being grateful for what you have, and you always find your life is less satisfying than someone else's. Your jealousy grows by regularly consuming other people's posts on social media too closely and this destructive habit makes you hate yourself even more.

6. You're afraid to fall in love.

Falling in love is something scary because it's very hard for you to be vulnerable with others. You don't want them to realize that you are not perfect because you can't even fully accept yourself. You always focus on your flaws instead of your strengths; thus it makes you believe that anyone will ever love you. It makes you close your heart from experiencing love.

7. You do regularly pity yourself.

When you hate yourself, self-pity will become a daily habit. You enjoy being sad and you complain a lot about your life. You always see your life as black and white, never in color, and you like to post those sad quotes everywhere, so people know just how sad you are. You tend to forget that you are the only one who can make yourself happy because everyone is busy saving themselves.

8. You're afraid of having big dreams.

Because you don't believe that you can achieve them. You always look down on yourself and it makes you afraid to go beyond your comfort zone. You hate the possibility of rejection and failure because those would make you feel worthless. Thus, you always hide in your shell and avoid those opportunities.

If we be honest, sometimes we're just not ready to forgive ourselves yet. There are no specific rules about how long it should take you to forgive yourself or when you should or shouldn't be ready. Understand that for as long as you are punishing yourself, you are suffering. Many people say that a person is healthiest when they treat themselves as their own best friend. Would you forgive your best friend if they hurt you? Consider that when struggling with whether you are ready to forgive yourself. Part of recovery and reaching self-acceptance is being compassionate with yourself about the stages of grief and change. For a person to change, things take time. Whether you are in the beginning phases of change or ready to do the hard work for forgiving, it is okay to be where you are at. Only you will know when you are truly ready.

There are some easy steps you can take if you are looking to forgive yourself.

1. Take full responsibility for whatever it is you have done.
2. Allow yourself to spend a little time in remorse but not to dwell in it.
3. Do what you can to make amends to whomever you have hurt, including yourself.
4. Focus on moving forward.

While these steps may seem simple enough, some pitfalls might happen along the way. These are perfectly normal. When looking to forgive yourself, you must be honest with yourself too. Some people will take responsibility for things they had no control over, leading them to follow unneeded steps for forgiveness. Ask yourself if you are responsible for whatever has happened, what role you played in it, and how much of your self-blame is justified. Until you are honest about these things, it will be difficult to put the past where it belongs.

Another thing to watch out for is getting stuck in a cycle of remorse. Try daily affirmations that you are a good person. Say this out loud and write down reasons you believe it to help combat the feelings of guilt and remorse that naturally come along with the journey of self-forgiveness. When working to make amends, be sure the other person wants it. If there are restraining orders, legal reasons, or even emotional reasons why it would be best not to contact the person you hurt, keep those in mind. You are better off skipping this step or writing a letter to the person and throwing it in the garbage can than triggering them with unwelcome contact. It might be therapeutic, though, to put yourself through the process of writing your remorse and feelings on paper even if you never let anyone else see those words but you.

When focusing on moving ahead, ask yourself what therapists call "the miracle question." That is, ask yourself what your life would look like if you were entirely comfortable with yourself and believed you were a good person. How would things be different? What changes would you make? How would those new behaviors and relationships feel? In answering these questions, you will have an outline of how to move forward.

Remember, go slow and easy with yourself. And if you feel like you can't do it alone, don't be afraid to reach out to a qualified mental health professional. They have the training and skills to walk you through the process of forgiveness. Even saying your story and feelings out loud will go a long way toward helping you move toward acceptance.

If you have never been to a therapist before and aren't sure what to expect, it's okay to ask questions. Things to consider might be to ask the therapist what kind of therapy they do and how long they have been in practice. You can learn a lot about a therapist ahead of time by reading their bio and learning about their background. Some psychologists are more hands-on than others. Some will tell you what they think you should do while others will encourage you to do that work yourself. Finding the right match for you will make a big difference in how long you are on your journey of self-forgiveness.

While it may feel overwhelming, we cannot rewrite the past, nor can we jump into another person's body for a clean slate. For those who are spiritual or religious, forgiveness and that fresh start could come simply by asking a higher power for it. But for those who don't think that's enough, it's important to remember that the only way through is forward. The future awaits and you deserve a second chance at happiness. Staying stuck in destructive cycles of guilt and resentment won't do much to help you accomplish your next best move.

For your best chance to leave the past in the past and move forward, write out a pros and cons list on what staying stuck versus total forgiveness could do for you. A complicated process? Yes. But the road after forgiveness is both clear and simple, living life at your best.

Sometimes the hardest thing for us to do after we've done something wrong is to forgive ourselves. We tend to be our own harshest critics, beating ourselves up long after others have forgiven us. Yes, repentance is important when we're in the wrong, but the Bible also reminds us that it's important to learn from our mistakes and move on. The book has much to say on the subject of self-forgiveness. Our God is a forgiving God. He is the first to forgive our sins and trespasses, and He reminds us that we must learn to forgive one another, too. Learning to forgive others also means learning to forgive ourselves.

1 John 1:9
"But if we confess our sins to him, he is faithful and just to forgive us our sins and to cleanse us from all wickedness."

Matthew 6:14-15
"If you forgive those who sin against you, your heavenly Father will

forgive you. But if you refuse to forgive others, your Father will not forgive your sins."

1 Peter 5:7

"God cares for you, so turn all your worries over to him."

Colossians 3:13

"Bear with each other and forgive one another if any of you has a grievance against someone. Forgive as the Lord forgave you."

Psalms 103:10-11

"He does not treat us as our sins deserve or repay us according to our iniquities. For as high as the heavens are above the earth, so great is his love for those who fear him."

Ephesians 4:32

"Let all bitterness and wrath and anger and clamor and slander be put away from you, along with all malice. Be kind to one another, tenderhearted, forgiving one another, as God in Christ forgave you."

Luke 17:3-4

"Take heed to yourselves. If your brother sins against you, rebuke him; and if he repents, forgive him. And if he sins against you seven times in a day, and seven times in a day returns to you, saying, 'I repent,' you shall forgive him."

Matthew 6:12

"Forgive us for doing wrong, as we forgive others."

Proverbs 19:11

"It's wise to be patient and show what you are like by forgiving others."

Luke 7:47

"I tell you, her sins—and they are many—have been forgiven, so she has shown me much love. But a person who is forgiven little shows only little love."

Isaiah 65:16

"All who invoke a blessing or take an oath will do so by the God of truth. For I will put aside my anger and forget the evil of earlier days."

Mark 11:25

"And whenever you stand praying, if you have anything against anyone, forgive him, that your Father in heaven may also forgive you your trespasses."

Matthew 18:15

"If another believer sins against you, go privately and point out the offense. If the other person listens and confesses it, you have won that person back."

CHAPTER SEVEN

Horizontal Forgiveness

Forgiveness is a moral and spiritual virtue in which the offended person tries, over time, to get rid of toxic anger or resentment and to offer goodness of some kind to the offending person. Reconciliation is not a moral virtue, but instead is a negotiation strategy in which two or more people come together again in mutual trust.

All moral virtues concern the inner quality of goodness and the possible outward manifestation of it. For example, the moral virtue of justice has the inner quality of knowing what it means to give people what they deserve and the outward manifestation of being fair. If you sign a contract with a bricklayer to pay $1,000 for a new wall to be built, you first have the inner intention to pay for the work. You then follow through outwardly when you exercise the virtue by paying the bricklayer once the work is done.

If the bricklayer, for some unexplainable reason, leaves the United States never to return, and gives no forwarding address, you do not then exercise the outward manifestation of justice. You do not pay the $1,000. Yet, you have exercised the moral virtue of justice because you have the inner quality of fairness and the intention to pay.

It is the same with forgiveness. You start with the inner quality of a motivation to rid yourself of resentment and the inner intention to be good, within reason, toward an offending person. If that person has no inner sorrow, never intends to apologize or to make amends, then you do not exercise the outward quality of forgiveness directly to that person. Yet, you still can have the intention to reconcile if the person substantially changes and the interactions become safe. You even can show an outward quality of forgiveness, for example, by not talking disparagingly about the offending one to other people.

In forgiveness, if a person continually verbally abuses you, you can have the inner quality of struggling to rid yourself of resentment as well as the inner quality of intending to be good to the other if that other substantially changes. Yet, if that person shows you by continued verbal abuse that there will be no apology, no making amends, then you do not exercise the outward quality of forgiving, at least not toward the person directly.

Suppose now that you decide to make the following rule for your life: I will not forgive if I cannot reconcile. What, then, are the implications for your own inner world, for your own psychological and spiritual health? As people forgive by exercising the moral virtue of forgiveness by trying to be good, within reason, toward an offending person, then the forgiver can reduce not only in anger but also in anxiety and depression and improve in self-esteem and hope. There are more reasons to forgive than this one, but this one can make a substantial difference to the forgiver's health.

Why would you not want to become healthier? If you reject forgiving because you conflate it with reconciliation, you may be inadvertently depriving yourself of a second chance at a healthy psychological life and even at a healthy relational life with others (not necessarily with the offending person). Deep anger from injustices can lead to a lack of trust in general, thwarting potentially uplifting relationships.

The offer of forgiveness can be unconditional, not at all dependent on the other's response of any kind, including an apology. Reconciliation, when at least one party is deeply and unfairly hurt, is conditional, dependent on how the offending party or parties understand their hurtful ways, change, and even apologize. How we think about forgiveness matters a great deal. If we make the philosophical error of equating forgiving and reconciling, then we are allowing the effects of an offending person to live within us for a long time, perhaps even for a lifetime if the psychological wounds are deep enough. Forgiving and reconciling are not the same. You are free to forgive, if you so choose, even if the other refuses to apologize.

Yes, we all know that the Bible is clear that Christians are to forgive others who sin against us, just as God has forgiven us for our sins (Matthew 6:14-15; Ephesians 4:32). However, there is a lot of misunderstanding in our culture about what that really means. So, we wanted to clarify what forgiveness is, why you should forgive, how to ask for forgiveness, and how to grant forgiveness to your spouse, friends, parents, or children. Because we are told to forgive "as the Lord has forgiven you" (Colossians 3:13), it can help to look at how God forgives us.

We have all sinned against God (Psalm 51:4; Romans 3:23). That sin creates a debt (Matthew 6:12); to make things right with God, we should have to pay for what we have done. That would be fair. Unfortunately, the fair payment for sinning against a holy God is death (Romans 6:23) and eternal separation from Him. Thankfully, wonderfully, God has eliminated that debt we owe, sending His Son to pay the penalty in our place (Mark 10:45). When we say we are forgiven by God, we mean that He no longer requires us to pay for our sins. Our debt is forgiven.

God's forgiveness is the model and motivation for how we are to forgive others (Matthew 18:23-35). He has freed you from a massive debt; in response, you should forgive the comparatively smaller debts that your spouse or other people owe you.

So, what does it mean to forgive someone? What does forgiveness look like in practice? Forgiveness is a canceling of debt. In a way, forgiveness is an accounting term; you forgive the debt and remove it from the ledger. In practice, that means you decide that you are not going to punish your spouse for what they have done or seek vengeance (Leviticus 19:18). You also won't intentionally seek to make them feel badly about it or bring it up in the future as a way to hurt them. The debt is gone—it's forgiven—so they no longer owe you. Forgiveness is a choice. You choose whether to forgive your spouse. It is an active decision you make, not a feeling that you passively experience. Because it is a choice, you can always offer forgiveness. Saying that you *can't* forgive someone really just means you *won't* forgive them—or that you simply misunderstand the meaning of forgiveness.

Forgiveness is for your benefit as well as theirs. Although we often think of forgiveness as a gift to the person being forgiven, it is really a gift you give yourself. Carrying a grudge only weighs you down. It might sometimes hurt your spouse, but it *always* affects you (Psalm 37:7-8; Ephesians 4:26). Forgiveness is not a feeling. You probably won't feel like forgiving your spouse when they have sinned against you. You will probably still feel hurt by their actions, at least for a while. However, forgiveness can help those feelings dissipate over time. Forgiveness is not forgetting. "Forgive and forget" is a nice sentiment, but you don't truly forget something. In fact, you might sometimes have to remind yourself that you have forgiven your spouse. You can choose not to bring it up or hold it against them, but you can't choose whether you will retain memories of the event.

Forgiveness is not waiting for them to pay you back. If your spouse has to make it up to you before you will forgive them, then that is not forgiveness at all; if they've repaid the debt, there is nothing left to forgive. Your spouse might choose to make amends after you forgive them, but that's their free choice, and cannot be a condition of true forgiveness. Forgiveness is not minimizing the sin or saying that it is OK for them to sin again. Forgiving your spouse doesn't mean that what they did wasn't hurtful or damaging to you. It's not a "free pass" for them to sin again because they know that you are going to forgive them (Romans 6:1-2). It just means that you're not the one who is going to extract justice (Romans 12:19).

Forgiveness is not necessarily letting them off the hook. There are times when it is wise to let someone experience the natural consequences of what they've done (Galatians 6:7-8). You should forgive them, but you don't have to shield them from those consequences. It may also be wise for them to have some restrictions going forward—rules, filters, or procedures that help prevent them from falling back into sin patterns. Forgiveness is not an instant conferral of trust. Trust is not a gift; it is earned over time. Forgiving your spouse just means that you are giving them an opportunity to regain trust by proving their faithfulness over a long season.

Forgiveness is not easy. Technically, and almost by definition, it is not fair; the fair thing would be for the offending party to pay restitution in full. But that's not how God treats us; His forgiveness of our sins is decidedly unfair in the most loving way possible (Romans 5:6-8). And that is why we should forgive each other.

Healing emotional wounds is a process of self-exploration, one that can provide endless benefits no matter what stage of life you are in. Resentment and self-loathing can be scarring if allowed to fester. Forgiveness is the best antidote for this toxicity, whether it's asking someone to forgive you, forgiving someone who has hurt you, or forgiving yourself. It's important to know that forgiveness isn't the same thing as wiping the slate clean. "Forgive" and "forget" are not helpful together. In order to move forward, you must recognize the truth of what happened. When you acknowledge what happened and accept that you can't change the past, you find the motivation to do something of value for yourself: forgive and heal.

Expressing your forgiveness directly to the person who hurt you isn't always necessary or possible. Forgiving someone is for your benefit, not theirs. The process of forgiveness and the release of thoughts and feelings that have kept you tied to the past can be done without the other person's participation. Forgiveness allows you to let go of the regrets or resentments that eat up your valuable energy. Before you can forgive, it's important to fully experience and let out the feelings tied to the emotional wound—anger, sadness, shame, fear, etc. Sometimes, writing a letter expressing how you feel can help you let go of negative emotions. You don't have to mail the letter. Burning it may feel better.

Forgiving yourself can be more difficult than forgiving someone else. It requires acknowledging what you did and recognizing the damage it did to yourself or others. For forgiveness to work, you have to recognize that you made a mistake—or many of them—and understand that if you knew then what you know now, you would have done things differently.

As they say, hindsight is 20/20. Situations, and the appropriate responses to them, are always clearer when looking back. The best you can do is accept what happened and make the best of the situation you're in now. Mindfulness can be useful in exploring why you did what you did. Gratitude can also be helpful because it allows you to move toward change. Atonement, making amends to the person you hurt or their symbolic representative, is a powerful way of moving toward self-forgiveness. If you take a realistic attitude about the weaknesses and imperfections of human beings, forgiving yourself and others may feel more comfortable. People make mistakes. We operate based on our own experiences and worldviews. We are all a mess of emotions and genetics.

When considering whether to forgive someone, it can be helpful to consider their life experiences. This doesn't mean excusing them for what they did. But the more you know about the forces that led to someone's choices and actions toward you, the more clearly you can see the inherent imperfection of being human.

For example, let's say your father left your family when you were young, and you just received a letter from him asking for your forgiveness. Would knowing the forces that drove his actions—his abandonment by his own father, his young age when he had you, his alcoholism—excuse his action? No, but it might make it easier to see his humanness and forgive him. Compassion and boundaries are not mutually exclusive, either. You can say both "I forgive you" and "I don't want you in my life." To forgive yourself and others, try to soften your stance on being human and understand that people are fallible. But also recognize that when people know better, they tend to do better. The self-exploration that leads to healing contains a lot of learning to know better. Letting go of resentments and regrets—in other words, practicing forgiveness— requires learning from and finding meaning in your emotional wounds.

You can transcend suffering by making meaning out of your hurt and learning what it has to teach you. You can make yourself better for having endured it, but first you must go through it. You have to accept, experience, process, and release to heal and come out stronger.

CHAPTER EIGHT

Vertical Forgiveness

Almost from birth, we are all thought to not be angry with God. We are convinced that such an emotional reaction to the ultimate Creator of all, could lead to us being struck down by lightning. It is in those moments that a toxic relationship begins. Let me clarify. It's not that we ourselves have a toxic relationship with God, but because of misunderstandings of scripture we have a toxic relationship with the way we've been taught to view God. There will never be any relationship that any of us could acquire that would be healthier than our relationships with God. What makes a healthy relationship? Honest. Freedom. Trust.

Well, how can we maintain an honest relationship with God if we cannot be honest with Him on the ways in which we feel he dropped the ball? Keep in mind that He never drops the ball, but in our humanized minds it can be difficult at times to return to a place of trusting Him when something so contrary to what we believe He had purposed for us occurs. So, what are we to do in those moments? Do we suck it up? Do we talk to everyone about it but Him? Trust me when I say this. There is no anger like spiritual anger. People live life everyday giving God the cold shoulder because they are angry with Him and either feel they'll do further damage to their lives by expressing such anger or they simply have no desire to reconcile their spiritual union with God. However, God never told us that we cannot be angry with Him. In fact, when we bring our feelings of confusion, anger, and fear to Him, it is sealing the intimacy of our relationship.

We all know what it is like to be angry, don't we? The emotion of anger is as common to humanity as sadness, love, and happiness. From the day we were born, we never had to be taught how to express our anger — it just came out. Even if you do not consider yourself to be an "angry person," everyone experiences anger at times.

In fact, we learn in the Bible that Jesus even felt anger! For example, in John 2 we see a side of Jesus that makes us a little uncomfortable because he had so much zeal for the house of God that he made a whip out of some cords to drive out a bunch of animals and the people selling them in the temple. Then he flipped over their tables and spilled their money out on the floor. The word "zeal" here means anywhere from excitement to fierceness and indignation. Considering how his zeal "consumed" him, I think we can say that he was a little more on the "angry" side than just "excited."

Later in John 11, we read about Jesus' reaction to the death of his friend, Lazarus. While the passage does not say that Jesus was angry necessarily, we do see that he was grieving so intensely that He (God in the flesh) actually wept. The phrases used to describe Jesus' grief in this passage depict a sense of great pain, deep movement, spiritual groaning, and emotional anguish that some Bible Dictionaries illustrate as a horse "snorting with anger."

So, while the emotion of anger is a natural response and even seen in Jesus himself, it means that it is not a sin by itself. This leads us to a question that many Christians wonder about: Is it wrong to be angry with God? To frame the answer to that question, we need to understand three realities about the emotion of anger which will provide insight into whether it is wrong to be angry with God. When we respond to a situation with anger, it shines a light on what we value and consider as right and wrong. On the other hand, if something does not produce any feelings of anger, we can conclude that it is not something we value that much.

When a situation turns out differently than we think it should have been, it naturally causes emotional friction in us that comes out as frustration, disappointment, annoyance, and anger. A child will get mad because he thought he *should have* gotten dessert. A teenager will get mad if she thinks her friend is treating her unfairly. An adult will get mad if someone or something they love is taken from them. In the example from John 2 earlier, Jesus felt angry because he had a high regard for God's house and knew that what was happening was wrong. So, if we find ourselves being angry with God, it reveals that we think God was unfair or did something wrong to us.

The best example of this is King David in 2 Samuel 6 when one of his men named Uzzah was killed by God because he touched the Ark of the Covenant to try to steady it when the oxen that were carrying it stumbled. As a result, David was not only unjustly upset with God, but it drove him to an unhelpful fear of God's wrath resulting in missing out on God's presence and blessing in Jerusalem for three months. We can also read some of David's laments to God in the Book of Psalms, such as when he cries out, "How long, O LORD? Will you forget me?" (Psalm 13:1-6). David wrongfully assumed that God had left or forgotten him, resulting in anger against him. So, if we are angry with God, we need to honestly ask ourselves what beliefs we have about God that are unscriptural, untrue, and unhelpful.

What we do with our anger is more important than just feeling it. While our anger might be a more subconscious emotional response, how we consciously react determines whether it is sin. That is why Paul told the believers in Ephesus to "be angry and do not sin…" (Ephesians 4:26). We all know that nothing good comes from anger (or any emotion) that is either uncontrolled or left bottled up. That is why parents teach their children how to calm themselves and deal with their anger in healthy ways. That is also why James instructs us to "be quick to hear, slow to speak, slow to anger" (James 1:19). Because it is not our anger itself that hurts others, it is how we react to the feeling with our words, attitudes, and actions.

In Numbers 20, Moses was so irate with the Hebrews for their rebellion and lack of faith that he acted out by striking a rock twice that God had only told him to tap. Interestingly, although Moses' anger-fueled disobedience was still effective in producing water from the rock. God punished Moses for his sinful action by declaring, "…Because you did not believe in me, to uphold me as holy in the eyes of the people of Israel, therefore you shall not bring this assembly into the land that I have given them" (Numbers 20:12).

So, even if our anger against God is wrongly placed, it only becomes sin when we react in a way that is sinful — by cursing God, by becoming bitter, by straying in our relationship with him, by hurting others, or by simply walking in disobedience. This leads to the final reality of our anger.

A mature believer will not stay angry. Instead of reacting in their anger in a way that is sinful, a mature person will consider why they are angry and will work to bridle, control, and even let go of their anger. To be serious, aggressive, and driven are all appropriate and effective at times, but acting *in* or being controlled by our anger will not produce healthy results. James even says that "for the anger of man does not produce the righteousness of God…" (James 1:20).

Paul goes as far as to say that if we are angry with a brother or sister in Christ that "…now is the time to get rid of anger… and forgive anyone who offends you. Remember, the Lord forgave you, so you must forgive others" (Colossians 3:8-13). So, if we are angry with God, how much more should we find the root cause in our heart and let it go. I do not think that God is upset with us when we are angry with him; I think he is sympathetic and merciful.

In the lamenting Psalms where David seems to be frustrated or even upset with God, he always ends up responding with praise and thankfulness instead of bitterness. For example, in Psalm 13:5-6 we read, "But I have trusted in your steadfast love; my heart shall rejoice in your salvation." Or in Psalm 42 after introspectively asking himself, "Why are you cast down, O my soul, and why are you in turmoil within me," David responds with "Hope in God; for I shall again praise him, my salvation and my God" (Psalm 42:11). What changed in David's heart? Not only did he let go of his feelings of anger against God but let go of his beliefs about God that were unhelpful, unscriptural, untrue, and wrongly placed. Instead, he confessed a common phrase in Scripture that God is "merciful and gracious... slow to anger... and abounding in steadfast love" (Psalm 86:15, 103:8, 145:8; Exodus 34:6; Number 14:18; Nehemiah 9:17).

What does it all mean? So, while we may not be sinning when we feel anger against God, we must use the emotion to drive us to look into our souls to discover a wrong belief, to surrender it to God, and then to turn and give God praise for how he is always good and what he does is always right, for his glory, and for our good. Let our anger drive us to a deeper love.

Signs of Being Angry with God:

Difficulty or reluctance when Praying:

> *"What's the point? God doesn't care anyways"*

Negative Thoughts and Expectations on Life:

> *"It'll never happen for me. Good things like that don't happen for me."*

No Testimony Zone:

"I don't want to hear it. I'm not in the mood to hear anyone talk about how good God is."

Nothing Makes Sense:

"If God had been here this wouldn't have happened." "Why do bad things happen to good people?" "I did exactly what God told me to do; now look at things!"

You can be angry with God and still do the following:

Go to Church (out of habit)

Pay your tithes (out of obligation)

Pray (Passive aggressive prayers)

Let's be honest. What is anger? Anger is just fear's little brother. We experience anger when something has frightened us. Often, we blame God for things His fan club did wrong. So, we can't go further without talking about the difference between Church Hurt and God Hurt. Church hurt can cut you to the core. Much like our parents, we see church leaders as having authority. We look to them to lead us and shepherd us well. We trust them with our hearts and with our areas of vulnerability. When the people whom we trust manipulate, shame, reject, or use others for selfish gain, the effects are extremely painful and confusing. It hits us where we are most tender, causing us to question both God and our own sense of worth. In some cases, the pain can cause you to wonder, *"If church can hurt me so deeply, then what does that say about God? Who is God anyway? Can He really be trusted?"*

In addition, church hurt can damage how you think about yourself. Rationally, you might know the pain is not your fault. But parts of you can still wonder if you did something wrong. Toxic shame enters your mind, and you might start wondering, *"If that church represents God, then how could they be wrong? What if I am the problem? What if I deserved what I got?"*

Church hurt is soul crushing. I'll be honest. The process of healing from church hurt is not easy. It can be hard to face the pain. It can be hard to disentangle the God who loves you from the misrepresentation of God by an unhealthy leader. Understandably, many people get angry and stay bitter. Others decide to leave the church all together. But I believe there is another way through. I have walked this path with countless individuals, and it is some of the most gratifying work that I do.

If you're struggling with the pain of church hurt or if a church misrepresented God to you through toxic, abusive actions or words, please know you are not alone. You are still in the center of God's love AND God's justice. God hates church hurt, too (See Matthew 18:6).

Here are four steps that I recommend healing from church hurt:

5 Steps to Heal from Church Hurt:

Step 1. Call a Thing a Thing: Define Church Hurt as Abuse

Church leaders hold power. But great power includes great responsibility. If someone misuses their power, the result is defined as "abuse," which means to act in a manner to cause "bad effect or for a bad purpose; misuse" (Oxford Languages Dictionary). Church hurt stems from experiencing someone else abusing their power. A church has the power to gather, encourage, and heal God's beloved people. On the positive side, church can help you:

- Encourage yourself and others (1 Thessalonians 5:11; Hebrews 10:25)
- Give thanks and marvel at God's wonders (Colossians 3:16)
- Grow in humble, honest self-awareness (James 4:8)
- Pray with other people (Acts 2:42)
- Grow in wisdom and knowledge of God (Ephesians 3:10)
- Care for those who are most vulnerable (James 1:27)

In contrast, when a church leader abuses his or her power, it has the opposite effect, such as causing:

- Discouragement and disappointment in yourself and others

- Feelings of anger, confusion, and bitterness toward God

- Toxic movement toward rigid self-denial and self-hatred

- Bypassing or denial of pain and emotions (vs. bringing them to God honestly)

- False ideas about God (vs. the God Jesus embodied)

- Further wounds on the most vulnerable

The first step toward healing, then, is to name the church hurt as "abuse." Here are some examples:

- He attacked the young girl that God made. *That was an abuse of church power.*

- She taught me I wasn't worthy of God's love. *That was an abuse of church power.*

- They told my secrets to others and called it prayer. *That was an abuse of church power.*

- He told me that my abusive husband's behavior was my fault. *That was an abuse of church power.*

- She said my depression was evidence that I lacked faith. *That was an abuse of church power.*

The purpose of this step is not to harbor resentment. Instead, the initial process of healing hinges upon you naming the wrong behavior that occurred.

Step 2. Separate the Church Hurt from God's Character

Some aspects of God's character are crystal clear throughout the Bible. If you feel busted up or beaten on by a church community, it is important to step back for a moment and remind yourself who God is apart from the hurtful actions. For instance:

- God loves justice, mercy, and humility. (Micah 6:8)

- God is for the poor in spirit, the grief-stricken, the humble, the broken-hearted, and the peacemakers (Matthew 5:1-12)

- God stands against the proud, and for the humble (James 4:6)

- God is love (1 John 4:7)

- God's presence shows up as love, joy, peace, patience, kindness, goodness, faithfulness, gentleness, and self-control (Galatians 5:22-23)

You might also look to the life of Jesus and notice how he interacted with various types of people. He was clear about his stance toward individuals in these three categories:

Abusers of Power:

Jesus gave his harshest words to religious leaders who judged, criticized, oppressed, and left people out. These folks created cliques and always attempted to maintain their power. If you're not convinced that Jesus was harsh with unhealthy religious leaders, read these passages: Matthew 23, Mark 9:42, Luke 11:43–44.

The Sufferers:

Jesus drew close to people who were hurting, wounded, sick, and suffering. He didn't blame them for their suffering, nor did he marginalize them. Instead, he encouraged them, helped them, and treated them with respect. Read some of the life-giving stories of how Jesus interacted with suffering in these passages: Luke 17:12–16, John 9:6–7.

The Marginalized:

Jesus also showed a soft spot for those on the outs, such as "sinners," rebels, and the people who others tended to despise. For example, do you remember the woman who got caught in adultery? Jesus purposefully intervened to protect her. In another story, Jesus first revealed his true identity to a woman four times divorced. She was from Samaria, a place equivalent to "the wrong side of the tracks." Read more stories of Jesus siding with marginalized individuals in these passages: Mark 2:15–16, Luke 7:36–39, John 4:25, 26.. As you identify God's desire to help hurting people, you will find a powerful ally. God is on the side of those who have suffered, not on the side of those who abuse their power.

Step 3. Recover Your Power

If you've experienced church hurt, it can cause you to feel helpless and alone. To reclaim your power, you need to set boundaries with those responsible for the pain. Then, you also need to heal the agony inside your own soul. But, in order to heal, you'll need the help of safe people. Here are some ways to start that process:

Prioritize your own emotional recovery first.

It's not your job to have empathy for those in power who hurt you. There might be a time for forgiveness and/or reconciliation way down the road. But it is far more important that you separate yourself out from the harm and restore the parts of yourself that were wounded.

Seek support outside of the church.

If your church culture is toxic, it's crucial to get a healthy perspective from someone who is outside that environment. For instance, contact a counselor or trusted adviser who can help you stay clear and grounded as you name the church hurt and find your way to solid ground.

Wait to communicate until you have a strong support network.

Once you are clear about the nature of your church hurt, you might try communicating boundaries with the leaders of a church community. But please do NOT take this step alone. It is wise to enlist help to ensure that you don't get pulled back up into a web of toxicity and experience more harm. If you do decide to confront a hurtful leader, make sure you have support. Then, pay close attention to the response. You will quickly learn if that person is messy-but-loving, or someone who is truly toxic. If it's the latter, it is probably time to find a new church community.

Step 4. Reclaim Your Spiritual Practices

As you begin to reclaim your personal power, you can also reclaim some spiritual practices. But, just like any physical wound, certain situations may rekindle more pain. With emotional pain, there may be specific words and practices that seem normal to everyone else, such as prayer or listening to a sermon, but they bring up uncomfortable, painful feelings within you. That's because those practices got twisted due to the leader's abusive actions.

For example, if someone betrayed your trust while claiming to "pray" for you, their actions could make the idea of prayer feel uncomfortable. Likewise, certain Bible verses may have been used to manipulate you, which might bring up painful feelings when you hear those passages again.

In those situations, notice the feelings and be gentle with your reaction. It doesn't mean that you don't love God. In fact, it's the opposite! You are developing important skills to help you discern when to trust versus when to sound the danger alarm. You're learning how to discover Jesus apart from the leaders who misrepresented him. You can reclaim your spiritual practices from the ones who stole them from you.

Turn the negative into a positive by redefining old harmful words into new terms. For example, think of "prayer" as just a loving way to talk with God. You could even keep your eyes open and look at something beautiful or comforting that reminds you of God's love. Talk to God out loud, listen to soothing music, walk with a friend, or write in a journal. When several people are gathered in meaningful, honest connection, God is there with them. Above all, God is against "church hurt."

God desires to meet you in the tender places and provide healing. He doesn't force, control, or manipulate. He wants to restore the goodness in your life that was taken away by an abusive leader. Begin your healing process by defining church hurt as abuse, separate the hurtful behavior from God's character, recover your personal power, and reclaim your spiritual practices. You are never alone in the miraculous power of God's love.

Finally. How do we heal and forgive God? Here is a list of steps that I recommend in your spiritual journey of healing:

1. God has given you permission to be angry. Now you must give yourself permission to be angry.

2. Make a list of what frightened you, not what angered you. Remember, anger is just derived from fear. You can get to the root of your anger so you can discover what frightened you.

3. Decide if you truly want to be aligned back with God.

4. Explain to God not "what He did" that frightened you, but "what it made you feel". There's a big difference.

5. Acknowledge that ultimately you are angry because God chose to teach a lesson with your life that you felt you did not need to learn.

6. Give yourself time to heal but seek God's forgiveness and forgive yourself. Because God is also inside of each of us, the most important step is to forgive ourselves for not being in control. Once you forgive yourself, you'll find the journey to forgiving God is quite simple.

Matthew 12:31-32

[31] *Wherefore I say unto you, All manner of sin and blasphemy shall be forgiven unto men: but the blasphemy against the Holy Ghost shall not be forgiven unto men.*

[32] *And whosoever speaketh a word against the Son of man, it shall be forgiven him: but whosoever speaketh against the Holy Ghost, it shall not be forgiven him, neither in this world, neither in the world to come.*

I cannot close without speaking on the unforgivable sin, of blasphemy. Let me begin by saying that I don't believe that Christians can blaspheme against the Holy Ghost. Once you truly believe, you believe. You cannot ever truly have an encounter with God and then doubt Him. Christians stand on a different side of Pentecost. We need to remember that we stand in a different position in redemptive history. The scribes who accused Jesus existed before Pentecost before the Spirit had been given in a new and definitive way. Now, the Spirit was always with God's people, always with Israel, was certainly with Jesus in a profound and meaningful way. In fact, Jesus presupposes that the Spirit was so well known that the scribe should have known better.

But we stand on a different side of Pentecost. We don't just *know* about the Holy Spirit. Believers are *born* of the Spirit, and they are *baptized* in the Spirit, and striving to be *filled* by the Spirit. Just as Satan cannot cast out Satan, as Jesus says to the scribes, the Spirit cannot commit blasphemy against the Spirit. If you are born of God—if you are baptized in the Spirit— I don't think you can commit this unforgivable sin, because we have the Pentecostal blessing of the Spirit *with us*.

The unforgivable sin is not a careless complaint but a calculated rejection. Blasphemy against the Holy Spirit is not some sort of careless complaint or some profanity you utter against God or God's spirit. We can look to the Bible itself for examples of complaints against God. Look at the Psalms or look at the book of Lamentations. These people make real complaints, real laments before God like, "God, where are you? Have you forgotten us? Have you gone on a holiday? Do you really know what you're doing?"

So, something you might say in a moment of anxiety, of desperation, or of fear, or of absolute despair when you weld as breaking around you—that is not blasphemy against the Holy Spirit, that's just talking to God and telling him what's on your heart, often in the most colorful way you can. But that's not what the scribes were doing. The scribes were the ones who claim to be the leaders of Israel. They'd been to the college of knowledge. They were experts in Hebrew law and its interpretation. What do they do? They look at the work of God in Christ, they look at the work of the Holy Spirit and God's Messiah—and they damn it all to hell.

And the reason they do that is not because they are careless, but because they calculated. They should have known what they were doing, and they have done the one thing for which there is no reprieve and no repentance. That's very different than your average Christian who's just crying out to God in despair or perplexion. The unforgivable sin results from a trajectory of spiritual hard-heartedness. Any person who has who is committed the unforgivable sin is someone who has reached a point of spiritual hardness that they are incapable of regret, incapable of remorse, incapable of sorrow for any moment of irreverence towards God. They have reached a point where they would not want forgiveness, where they do not want anything of God.

On the contrary, a person who has cried out to God or even against God in anxiety, or despair, or just wondering, but then feels some measure of regret for that, knowing they have been less than worshipful or thankful to the heavenly father, or to the Lord Jesus, or to the Spirit. That's fundamentally different!

CHAPTER NINE

"It (Forgiveness) Is Finished"

I can truly say that I am a testament of forgiveness. I have experienced the wonderful forgiveness of God and man, and I have finally been able to return that gift back to the world. Yes, again, I did call forgiveness a gift. I lost many years of my life struggling with so many issues that I had no idea were rooted in unforgiveness. Many of us still work, lead families, pastor, lead companies, and serve in our communities with mountains of unforgiveness traveling with us on our backs every single day. We may not realize it in the moment, but all of that unforgiveness is in fact influencing all of our decisions. It becomes a part of us. It was a part of me. It remained a part of me, until I spoke it as Christ spoke it, "It is Finished." It was finished.

The Cross of Jesus Christ is the most precious emblem to those of us who call Jesus the Lord of our lives. We love the Cross and cherish it because of the price that was paid 2,000 years ago when Jesus died for our sins. The Cross represents our forgiveness, our freedom, our redemption. We love it so much that we adorn our churches and homes with crosses, and women even wear them around their necks. But when the pure Lamb of God hung on that Cross, we deem so precious - naked, beaten, and bleeding profusely before a watching world - it was a ghastly sight. Indeed, it was the most horrendous moment in human history.

No death was more scandalous than death on a cross. Such a death was dreadful and hideous, designed to discredit and tarnish the memory of the one dying. Blood drenched Jesus' torso, pouring from His head and brow, running like rivers from the deeply torn flesh in His hands and feet. The effect of the scourging that Jesus had received in Pilate's palace began to take its toll as His body swelled up and became horribly discolored. His eyes were matted with the blood that poured from the wounds in His brow - wounds caused by the crown of thorns that bore down into His skull as the soldiers pushed it hard upon His head. The whole scene was ugly, unsightly, repulsive, sickening, vile, foul, and revolting.

In the Jewish world, nakedness was a particularly profound shame. Because the body was made in the image of God, the Jewish people believed it was a great dishonor to display a naked body. So as if Jesus' suffering had not already been enough, He experienced the ultimate act of degradation and shame as He hung on the Cross, naked and exposed before all those who watched the unfolding drama.

Approximately 700 years earlier, the prophet Isaiah correctly prophesied Jesus' appearance on the Cross. In Isaiah 52:14, the prophet wrote with a sense of horror, "As many were astonished at thee; his visage was so marred more than any man, and his form more than the sons of men." In Isaiah 53:2, Isaiah continued, "…He hath no form nor comeliness; and when we shall see him, there is no beauty that we should desire him."

Jesus had been put through horrendous forms of torture and had been atrociously abused and battered. As a result, "…His face and His whole appearance were marred more than any man's and His form beyond that of the sons of men…" (Isaiah 52:14 *AMP*). In the *New International Version*, this verse is translated to say, "…His appearance was so disfigured beyond that of any human being and his form marred beyond human likeness.…"

In Isaiah 53:3-5, Isaiah continued to vividly describe Jesus' sacrifice. He wrote, "He is despised and rejected of men; a man of sorrows and acquainted with grief: and we hid as it were our faces from him; he was despised, and we esteemed him not. Surely, he hath borne our griefs, and carried our sorrows: yet we did esteem him stricken, smitten of God, and afflicted. But he was wounded for our transgressions, he was bruised for our iniquities: the chastisement of our peace was upon him; and with his stripes we are healed."

When Jesus died on that Cross:

- He bore our griefs.

- He carried our sorrows.

- He was wounded for our transgressions.

- He was bruised for our iniquities.

- He was chastised for our peace.

- He was scourged for our healing.

As Jesus approached death, the Bible tells us, "They gave him vinegar to drink mingled with gall…." (Matthew 27:34). As we saw in Chapter 25, a man who was to be executed could request a narcotic, mingled together with wine, which would help alleviate the pain of his execution. As noted before, the word "gall" in this verse is a special Greek word that refers to a painkiller that was mingled together with wine.

John 19:28-30: Jesus knew that his mission was now finished, and to fulfill Scripture he said, "I am thirsty." A jar of sour wine was sitting there, so they soaked a sponge in it, put it on a hyssop branch, and held it up to his lips. When Jesus had tasted it, he said, "It is finished!" Then he bowed his head and gave up his spirit.

That phrase is actually the translation of one word, "tetelestai," in the original language of the Bible. And this rich and carefully chosen word is full of powerful meaning.

Let's explore some of the facets of this word's significance.

1. Tetelestai – The Work Is Complete

This was Jesus' exclamation that He had finished the work the Father had sent Him to do. The work having been fully completed, Jesus bowed His head and died. One writer has noted that when a servant was sent on a mission and then later returned to his master, he would say, "Telelestai," meaning, "I have done exactly what you requested" or "The mission is now accomplished."

In that moment when Jesus cried out, he was exclaiming to the entire universe that He had faithfully fulfilled the Father's will and that the mission was now accomplished. No wonder Jesus shouted ¾ for this was the greatest victory in the history of the human race! He had been faithful to His assignment even in the face of unfathomable challenges. But now the fight was over, and Jesus could cry out to the Father, "I have done exactly what You asked Me to do!" or "The mission is accomplished!"

In New Testament times, when an employee had completed a day's work or finished a project, he would tell his boss "tetelestai." This was to signal that whatever it was that he was assigned to do was now completed. Similarly, when an artist would complete a piece of art, he would have a moment of unveiling where he would declare "tetelestai." This too was to signal that his masterpiece was complete. No more touch-ups or adjustments are necessary, the work is done. When Jesus came to this world, he told us what his job was: to provide salvation to a lost and broken world.

Luke 19:10: For the Son of Man came to seek and save those who are lost.

So, in his last words, Jesus was communicating that the work he came for was accomplished. The task of earning the salvation of the world was completed in his work on the cross. No more additions or adjustments were necessary – salvation was completed.

2. Tetelestai – The Sacrifice Is Accomplished

The word tetelestai was the equivalent of the Hebrew word spoken by the high priest when he presented a sacrificial lamb without spot or blemish. Annually the high priest entered the Holy of Holies, where he poured the blood of that sacrificial spotless lamb on the mercy seat of the Ark of the Covenant. The moment that blood touched the mercy seat, atonement was made for the people's sins for one more year ¾ when once again, the high priest would enter beyond the veil of that sacred room to offer blood. This was done year after year to obtain the annual, temporary forgiveness of sin.

But when Jesus hung on the Cross, He was both Lamb and High Priest. In that holy moment as our Great High Priest, Jesus offered His own blood for the permanent removal of sin. He offered up the perfect sacrifice of which every Mosaic sacrifice was a type and symbol - and in that instant, there remained no more need of offering for sin.

Jesus entered the Holy Place and offered His own blood - a sacrifice so complete that God never again required the blood of lambs for forgiveness. As Hebrews 9:12 says, "Neither by the blood of goats and calves, but by his own blood he entered in once into the holy place, having obtained eternal redemption for us."

Thus, when Jesus said, "It is finished!" He was declaring the end of sacrifice because the ultimate Sacrifice had finally been made! Atonement was completed, perfected, and fully accomplished. It was done once and for all - finished forever!

Every Jewish person there would have instantly recognized *Tetelestai* as the equivalent of a Hebrew phrase that was used in the Old Testament sacrificial system. Each year, on the Jewish holiday called The Day of Atonement, the High Priest would enter the temple and make a special sacrifice for the sins of the people of Israel. As soon as the priest had killed the animal, he would emerge from the place of sacrifice and declare to the waiting crowd "it is finished" in Hebrew. In this sacrifice, all the sins of Israel were symbolically placed on the lamb that was killed and punished in their place. Yet the Bible teaches that this sacrificial system was never complete or finished because the sacrifice of that lamb was imperfect and temporary. But when Jesus died on the cross, he became the perfect and final sacrifice for all sin. The Book of Hebrews describes how Jesus was the ultimate Lamb of God and by his sacrifice, the work of forgiveness was finally complete.

3. Tetelestai – The Debt Is Paid in Full

Maybe the most common use of "tetelestai" in Jesus' day was in debt collecting. When a person finally paid off a loan, they were issued a receipt that was stamped with the word "tetelestai" which meant that their debt was now paid in full. This was verification that they were no longer responsible for any of that debt, that everything they owed was completely and permanently paid for. The Bible says that our sin created a debt to God, and one that we could never pay back on our own. But when Jesus died, he was paying off our debt of sin once and for all. Again, the Book of Hebrews describes the finality of Jesus' payment for our sin.

When a debt had been fully paid off, the parchment on which the debt was recorded was stamped with tetelestai, which meant the debt had been paid in full. This means that once a person calls Jesus the Lord of His life and personally accepts His sacrifice, no debt of sin exists for that person any longer. The debt is wiped out because Jesus paid the price for sin that no sinner could ever pay. Jesus took our place. He paid the debt of sin we owed. And when we by faith repent and receive Him as Lord, we are set free! This is why Paul wrote, "In whom we have redemption through his blood, even the forgiveness of sins" (Colossians 1:14)

When Jesus uttered those words, "It is finished!" it was His declaration that the debt was fully satisfied, fulfilled, and complete. His blood utterly and completely cleansed us forever. It was far-reaching and all-embracing for all of us who put our faith in Him.

Hebrews 10:12-13, 18: But our High Priest offered himself to God as a single sacrifice for sins, good for all time. Then he sat down in the place of honor at God's right hand...And when sins have been forgiven, there is no need to offer any more sacrifices.

4. It Is Finished

In classical Greek times, the word tetelestai depicted a turning point when one period ended, and another new period began.

When Jesus exclaimed, "It is finished!", it was indeed a turning point in the entire history of mankind, for at that moment the Old Testament came to an end - finished and closed - and the New Testament began. The Cross was "the Great Divide" in human history. When Jesus cried out, "It is finished!" He was shouting that the Old Covenant had ended, and the New Covenant had begun!

In that divine moment when Jesus cried, "It is finished," all the Old Testament prophecies about Jesus' earthly ministry were fulfilled. The justice of God had been fully met and satisfied by the Lamb of God. At that moment, the sacrifices of the Old Testament permanently ceased, for the perfect Sacrifice had laid down His life for the salvation of mankind. Jesus' mission was accomplished. Thus, He could cry out that His task was complete!

Never forget that because Jesus was willing to offer His own blood for the full payment of our sinful debt, we are forgiven and utterly debt-free. "PAID IN FULL" has been stamped on our past sinful record because Jesus paid the price for our redemption with His own blood.

Isaiah said, "Surely he hath borne our griefs, and carried our sorrows: yet we did esteem him stricken, smitten of God, and afflicted. But he was wounded for our transgressions, he was bruised for our iniquities: the chastisement of our peace was upon him; and with his stripes we are healed" (Isaiah 53:4,5). So, remember:

- If you are consumed with grief, remember that Jesus bore *your* grief.

- If you are overwhelmed with sorrows, remember that He carried *your* sorrow.

- If you are trapped in a life of transgression, remember that He was wounded for *your* transgressions.

- If you are living in sin, you can be forgiven because He was bruised for *your* iniquities.

- If you are tormented and have no peace, remember that He was chastised for *your* peace.

- If you are physically or mentally sick, remember that He was wounded for *your* healing.

Jesus paid the price for your salvation, for your liberation, for your physical healing, and for your complete restoration. When the price for your forgiveness was complete, Jesus bowed His head and died. God's justice had been fulfilled. The Old Covenant had ended, and the New Covenant had begun. It was the fulfillment of one and the beginning of another.

Think of the price Jesus paid and what His death accomplished for you. Doesn't it make you want to stop for a few minutes to thank Him for what He has done for you? Where would you be today if Jesus had not died on the Cross for you? Why don't you take a little time right now to express your heartfelt thanksgiving to Jesus for paying the debt you never could have paid!

All of these nuances of tetelestai converge together to communicate a beautiful truth – that Jesus completed the work of salvation once and for all. That means it is not up to us to add anything, complete anything, finalize anything when it comes to our salvation – Jesus did it all. So now, when we have put our trust in the finished work of Jesus, we can rest in confidence of our salvation and pursue God with our whole hearts.

Forgiving others will rarely be as easy as breathing or blinking. Let's be real. If forgiveness for man required Christ's bloody sacrifice, then what would make us think that we wouldn't have to bear some cross in forgiving one another as well? Now THANKFULLY, we don't have to be subjected to the extremities that Christ subjected Himself to for forgiveness of man, but we will have to pull on God in the same likeness to get us through the other side of our pain.

It takes work and intentionality to begin – and end – the process of forgiveness. But how can we tell when the process is over? Is forgiveness ever over? The journey to (and through) forgiveness takes time;

it processes us through many phases – from hate, anger, denial, acceptance and back again. I believe there is a point where the process of forgiveness is complete. In my own journeys to forgiveness, the following signs have helped me to measure if I have forgiven:

1. When you can speak of the offense from a point of reference vs. a point of pain

When you talk about what "they did", is your context one of reference or reliving the painful situation? When we reference a past event, we simply state that the event happened. We know we're reliving a situation if we speak about it, and it evokes all of its negative emotions and energy around the subject.

The ability to reference vs. relive a hurtful event doesn't just fall out of the sky. But, as forgiveness matures in your heart, you will be able to feel less and less pain regarding the incident, until one day you can speak that "it happened" vs. internalizing "the pain that happened to me".

2. When revenge, payback, retaliation becomes a non-issue.

"Get 'em, Jesus!" How many can raise their hand in transparency, that you wanted some extreme evil, some deadly disease or misfortune to happen to the one who hurt you? Lord Jesus, please forgive and heal our revenge-like nature!

With hand raised, I can say that when you honestly and truthfully wish the person the best, when you hope no harm comes to them, when they no longer have to pay penance for what they did, your forgiveness has reached a beautiful milestone of completeness.

3. When you've stopped hiding behind "I let it go."

Letting go is absolutely a part of forgiveness. But, how many of our "let go's" are simply a feeble attempt to avoid conflict and/or bury the pain?

I remember my carefully crafted masks of "that doesn't bother me anymore" and "I'm really not phased." All lies! If you're committed to the forgiveness process and honest with yourself, you'll eventually learn that buried pain does not equal forgiveness. Hiding unforgiveness behind denial will only prolong your pain and stunt your healing. It takes work to honestly "let it go", and when you do, the pain will no longer claw its way back to the surface.

4. When you can fully accept that God loves the offender just as much as He loves you.

Depending on the offense, sometimes it's hard to comprehend how God can love someone who did something so horrible to us. Remember that God will never forsake others in loyal response to our hurt. God is loyal only to his Word (Psalms 138:2); God is not tempted with evil (James 1:13).

At the onset of our pain, we deem ourselves "higher, or better" than the person who offended us. But, as we walk through forgiveness, our sense of self in relation to the offender miraculously evens out. We're able to own that we ourselves have done wrong and that we all need God's love and forgiveness – who gives it freely to us all.

Now, the signs above should not be confused with when to trust a person again. I fully believe that you can forgive someone completely without allowing yourself to trust them again or give them close access to your heart.

CHAPTER TEN

The Season of The Unstoppable

Imagine that at your first birthday party, your mom gave you a large pair of purple shades to shield your eyes. With purple frames and purple lens, you wore the shades religiously your entire childhood. You slept with the shades on. You are with the shades on. Perhaps you even played with your friends and attended school with the purple shades on. Then imagine one day that someone removes your shades from your eyes leaving you to realize a shocking discovery.

Trauma is like wearing purple shades. As long as we have untreated trauma and unforgiveness we go throughout life wearing purple shades, and everything that we see is purple. Yes, there's a dog, but it's a purple dog. Yep, there's the sun, but it's a purple sun. Yep! I see the grass, but it's purple grass. You never quite notice just how much unforgiveness tainted your views and perspectives on life until you heal and forgive. You'd be surprised of all the ways you could have seen, heard, or experienced God had you not lost such time wearing purple shades.

Matthew 5:8 *"Blessed are the pure in heart for they shall see God"*

What is meant by pure in heart? If we reflect on scriptures, then we must settle upon the idea that "pure" does not mean perfect or without sin as Christ already died for our sins. Pure refers to a heart that models the heart of Christ, which is a forgiving heart. It is only those who have the ability and willingness to forgive that will see God.

I have spent many decades in the ministry. I am a husband. I am a father, a brother, and a friend. I am a pastor. I wear many hats, but I have had my share of moments that gave me reasons that I felt justified me not having a pure heart. I spent time on the streets. I spent times questioning myself and others. I had trust issues and I had anger issues, but I always had God. Let me explain. I always had God. Even when I didn't feel that I had Him because of the impurities of my heart, I still had Him. I always felt a higher calling for more. More love? More service? More preaching? More leading? More forgiveness. It was only when I found the power of spiritual alignment that rested within forgiveness that I felt as if I was able to see God in a way that I never knew existed. I never knew that He could speak so clearly and walk so closely to me while I was still here in this mortal flesh. He did, and He has continued to walk next to me. It isn't because I am so faithful, obedient, or perfect, it is because I found the commonality between being one with His son. I found my willingness to forgive, and it freed me.

Brothers and sisters, God freed me in ways that I didn't know freedom could exist and all because of forgiveness. Yes. Forgiveness.

You see, forgiveness is our way of honoring Christ's sacrifice. Forgiveness is an opportunity to partake in communion every day and remember the death, burial, and resurrection of our Lord and Savior, Jesus Christ. You see, once you get that first glance of God that was spoken of in Matthew 5:8, you cannot go back to that purple lens of pain. You cannot go back to being a half once you know what it is like to be whole with the Creator.

I no longer give anyone the authority to sabotage my alignment with God. The truth is that they never had the authority anyways. It is important that you understand that after forgiveness comes freedom, and after freedom comes FAVOR! God is saving the best for last. We are the ones who are going to experience the favor of God in its fullness. Get ready because there are going to be some changes around your house - favor is coming!

"Thou shalt arise and have mercy upon Zion: for the time to favour her, yea, the set time, is come" (Ps. 102:13).

Notice the Psalmist said the set time is come. I believe that this is a key phrase. A "set time" would indicate that God's already programmed it in and no devil, or man, or government can change it. It is a set time. Notice what this "set time" is for: Favor to come upon Zion. Zion is always symbolic of the church. In other words, there is a set time for favor to come upon the church like it has never experienced before. Please understand that the Psalm is prophetic.

Remember we're reading the words of a prophet, not just a king, nor just a psalmist. He's seeing into the future. Verse 15 says, So the heathen shall fear the name of the Lord and all the kings of the earth thy glory.

The "ages to come" that Paul spoke about in Ephesians 2:7 have come. Therefore, we should expect the favor of God on us like never before.

Favor Produces Wealth

"Lift up shine eyes round about, and see: all they gather themselves together, they come to thee: thy sons shall come from far, and thy daughters shall be nursed at thy side.

"Then thou shall see, and flow together, and shine heart shall fear, and be enlarged; because the abundance of the sea shall be converted unto thee, the forces of the Gentiles shall come unto thee" (Isa. 60:4-5).

In the Hebrew, the word "forces" is translated "wealth." Wealth is associated or connected to favor. If you study your Bible, you'll see that many who walked in the favor of God experienced financial blessings as well. Favor produces wealth.

We know that God has prophesied that a financial inversion will take place in the earth before the appearing of the Lord Jesus, and that the wealth of the sinner has been laid up for the just. So, if this "set time" of favor has come, then the church can anticipate greater wealth and finances. It will be experienced by those who are faithful and living righteously according to the Word of God. If you are one of those, then you are a candidate for greater finances than you've ever experienced before in your life.

Of course this only applies to tithers. If you aren't a tither, then He's certainly not going to cause this financial inversion to come on you. But on the other hand, if you are a tither, then get ready because He's going to pile it on those He can trust!

I want you to see a pattern for this in 2 Chronicles 1:12 when Solomon was given the assignment to build the temple:

"Wisdom and knowledge is granted unto thee; and I will give thee riches, and wealth, and honor, (or favor) such as none of the kings have had that have been before thee, neither shall there any after thee have the like"

God is saying, "I'm about to put favor on you like no one before you has ever walked in."

"And the king made silver and gold at Jerusalem as plenteous as stones..." (2 Chron. 1:15)

Later in 2 Chronicles we see that the Lord appears in His glory:

"It came even to pass, as the trumpeters and singers were as one, to make one sound to be heard in praising and thanking the Lord: and when they lifted up their voice with the trumpets and cymbals and instruments of music and praised the Lord, saying, For he is good; for his mercy endureth for ever: that then the house was filled with a cloud, even the house of the Lord; So that the priests could not stand to minister by reason of the cloud for the glory of the Lord had filled the house of God" (2 Chron. 5:13,14).

"... the time to favour her, yea, the set time, is come.... When the Lord shall build up Zion, he shall appear in his glory" (Ps. 102:13,16).

Notice what precedes the appearing of the Lord: a "set time of favor." We just read about a pattern for that when Solomon built the temple. Notice God granted him honor and favor and with it came riches, wealth, and honor. Not only that, but with it came the right people, all that he needed, abundance, plenty, expertise, quality, talent, and anointing. I submit to you that we are in that set time and that's what we can expect.

Can you imagine how exciting this is going to be as we lay hold of it and begin to walk in it? God is saving the best for last. Now, I want to give you 10 major benefits that I've discovered from the Word of God to those who walk in God's divine favor. These are benefits you can expect when the favor of God is on your life.

Study each of these carefully and begin to confess them every day. God confirms His Word when we are bold to declare it.

8 Rewards of the Favor of God

1. Favor produces supernatural increase and promotion.
"But the Lord was with Joseph, and shewed him mercy, and gave him favour in the sight of the keeper of the prison" (Gen. 39:21).

2. Favor produces restoration of everything that the enemy has stolen from you.
"And I will give this people favour in the sight of the Egyptians: and it shall come to pass, that, when ye go, ye shall not go empty" (Ex. 3:21).

3. Favor produces honor in the midst of your adversaries.
"And the lord gave the people favour in the sight of the Egyptians. Moreover, the man Moses was very great in the land of Egypt, in the sight Pharaoh's servants, and in the sight of the people" (Ex 11:3).

4. Favor produces increased assets, especially in the area of real estate.
"And of Naphtali he said, O Naphtali, satisfied with favour, and full with

the blessing of the Lord, possess thou the west and the south" (Deut. 33:23).

5. Favor produces great victories in the midst of great impossibilities.

"For it was of the Lord to harden their hearts, that they should come against Israel in battle, that he might destroy them utterly, and that they might have no favour, but that he might destroy them, as the Lord commanded Moses" (Josh. 11:20).

6. Favor produces recognition, even when you seem the least likely to receive it.

"And, Saul sent to Jesse, saying, Let David, I pray thee, stand before me; for he hath found favour in my sight" (1 Sam. 16:22).

7. Favor produces prominence and preferential treatment.

"And the king loved Esther above all the women, and she obtained grace and favour in his sight more than all the virgins; so that he set the royal crown upon her head and made her queen instead of Vashti" (Est. 2:17).

8. Favor produces petitions granted even by ungodly civil authorities.

"If I have found favour in the sight of the king, and if it please the king to grant my petition, and to perform my request, let the king and Haman come to the banquet that I shall prepare for them, and I will do tomorrow as the king hath said" (Est. 5:8).

So, these are 8 major rewards that I've seen in my study of the Favor of God! The Psalmist says that we are compassed about by the favor of God. One translation says, "It surrounds us." When you get up every morning, anticipate the favor of God going before you. Anticipate the favor of God surrounding you. Expect favor to open doors every day because of your willingness to practice forgiveness. Expect these rewards to manifest in your life.

Remember you will get exactly what you expect. If you expect God's favor to surround you, then you will see it. If you don't, then it won't. Your expectations are more powerful than any negative thing that Satan can put before you. They will override the negative no matter how often they may manifest in your life. So, expect God's favor in your life and watch what it will do. The set time has come so tap into it!

Tapping into that power and favor will usher you into the season of the unstoppable. My power and anointing in God was unstoppable because my willingness to align with Christ and grant forgiveness was also unstoppable.

With that in mind, I want to give you a few examples of humans who surrendered to God and who became UNSTOPPABLE.

1. **Joseph was UNSTOPPABLE**. 10 ruthless brothers, a sex-hungry wife, and years in prison could not stop Joseph. After 20 years his dream came to pass, and he told his brothers that God had taken what they planned for evil and turned it around for his good.

2. **David was UNSTOPPABLE**. An angry king with a cold-blooded army could not stop David. Time after time Saul attempted to have David killed, but God protected him for his purpose. After 13 years God's words spoken to him through the prophet Samuel came to pass and David became king.

3. **Gideon was UNSTOPPABLE**. 125,000 Soldiers could not stop Gideon and his 300. It wasn't a fair fight because God was on Gideon's side. You + God = Victory, every time! God caused the enemy to turn on themselves and kill each other, all because Gideon was doing what God called him to do.

4. **Paul was UNSTOPPABLE**. Floggings, stonings, shipwrecks and imprisonments could not stop Paul. Paul's attitude was, "For me to live is Christ." It's like the enemy said, "Okay Paul, well, if you say, 'To live is Christ," then we are going to kill you." Paul said, "That's okay, because for me, to die is gain." The enemy then said, "Okay Paul, in that case, we are not going to kill you, nor will we let you live in peace." To which Paul said, "That's okay too! For I reckon that the sufferings of this present time are

not worthy to be compared with the glory which shall be revealed in us!" In other words, Paul said, "If you let me live, I'll serve the Lord.

If you kill me, I'll go on to heaven. If you make me suffer, I'll have a bigger crown when I get there. Bottom line: there's nothing you can do to stop me!"

5. **Jesus was UNSTOPPABLE**. Satan could not stop Jesus. The Bible tells us that if the princes of this world would have known what they were doing they would have never crucified the Lord of Glory. When they were killing Jesus, they thought they were winning, but they were actually losing. When the first drop of blood hit the ground, it sealed Satan's fate.

6. **YOU are UNSTOPPABLE**. If Satan knew any better, he would leave you alone. He can't stop God's purpose. Satan cannot stop a man or woman of God who is walking in their divine assignment. That's why he wants to get you frustrated. When you get frustrated, YOU QUIT. Satan cannot stop you, but you can stop yourself when you quit.

So, my message to you is... NEVER GIVE UP, NEVER CAVE IN, and NEVER QUIT! The only way you can lose is if you quit. Say, "I will not lose, because I refuse to quit! I will not quit because I will not stop honoring the works of Christ. I will forgive. I will forgive as Christ forgave. There is peace, joy, and favor in forgiveness. There is freedom in forgiveness"

The End

About Apostle J.Q. Lockett

Apostle J.Q. Lockette is a native of New Haven, Connecticut. At an early age, he realized a tremendous call of God on his life. Much of his youth was spent in prayer and seeking the God's face for clarification of this call. At the age of 15, he was licensed as a minister at Bible Gospel Center in New Haven, Connecticut where the late John A. Good was Pastor.

After high school, he moved to Atlanta, Georgia to attend Morehouse College, where he later graduated. During the early 90s, he joined New Life Christian Center, under the leadership of the late Bishop Gus Kilgore of Eatonton, Georgia. There is where the mantle of God was released, and he was confirmed to the Office of the Prophet. Since 1991 until now, he remains the Pastor of Grace Church of Stone Mountain in Stone Mountain, Georgia

He was later affirmed as an Apostle and sat under the direction and leadership of the late, Apostle Robert Evans, Jr. Grace Church and Apostle Lockette served under the apostolic covering of Chief Apostle Janice L. Dillard of Ft. Lauderdale, Florida.

Apostle Lockette is a man of great vision and uncompromising faith. He also birthed out an organization, Miracle Revival Assemblies Fellowship International (MRA). MRA is a fellowship of pastors with like minds, who come together to break down cultural and denominational barriers to win souls for the Kingdom of God. It is also pastoral training ground with a strong emphasis on a life of integrity and accountability, helping ministry leaders to effectively balance family and ministry.

Because of his electrifying style of preaching, Apostle Lockette is declared a preacher's preacher. His known as "God's Man of Faith and Power," as he ministers the gospel under a fresh and viable anointing with an accurate and powerful prophetic utterance. By the grace of God, and with an eye single to His glory, Apostle Lockette has been favored to travel extensively and preach the gospel of Jesus Christ across the country. His desire is to see the Body of Christ come into full maturity and fulfill its purpose.

Following his endeavors in the Kingdom, his chief joys are his beautiful wife, Dr. Hashonah who stands beside him in ministry as Executive Pastor, and three wonderful children, son Nicholas Royale, two daughters, Jade Shoshana and Amber Quinelle. Apostle is also grateful to God for his granddaughters, Jayden Ambria, and J'adore Armani and his only grandson, Khalil Quinn.

CPSIA information can be obtained
at www.ICGtesting.com
Printed in the USA
BVHW070434190922
647080BV00005B/18